WE ARE ALL A WORK IN PROGRESS

For more information, please visit
www.weareallaworkinprogress.co.uk/contact

First edition

ACKNOWLEDGEMENTS

Before we start, some heartfelt thanks.

Before the book was ready to be published, I was very lucky to have the support, help and advice of some amazing friends.

They read the drafts, they gave me feedback and suggestions, some even undertook the proofreading. All of their time and energy is very gratefully received and so I start this book with a very special mention to the following people:

Jo, Harry, Sarah, Mandy, Val, Jill, James, Paul, Mincer (Francis/Gary), Helen, Karen, Sherrie, Sally, Angela, Kat, Lisa and Rosa.

The wonderful author picture was taken by my dear friend Maz at https://www.professionalrebel.co.uk/

You are all total stars and I send you much love and my deepest gratitude for your help.

Jo, July 2021

CONTENTS

INTRODUCTION

Why I decided to write this book

Whenever I feel overwhelmed or worried, I tend to reach for old faithful ways of handling whatever it is that has come up. I think we all do this naturally. However, some of the ways I identified as 'handling' things were actually really damaging or expensive, or both. When I started to think about this, I wasn't sure they did actually help, perhaps they did at the time, but not in the longer term. The 'other' ways that I relied upon were really easy, useful and actually helped me – but where had these positive solutions come from? And how did I have so many? A lot of them were free and only needed a notepad and pen, in fact the majority would be useless without those two items, so as long as I had access to paper – highly likely, and a pen, also very probable, the free and easy solutions were available at a moment's notice.

I was reading *Help Me! One woman's quest to find out if self-help really can change her life* by Marianne Power. I loved this book. I recommended it to friends who also loved it. Power set out to read twelve self-help books in a year and report on how she found them. This made me realise that I have actually read, listened to, studied and absorbed many, many titles over the years and I have created a stockpile of ideas and methods that I draw upon again and again when I am stuck, overwhelmed, unhappy or worried about something. It's all in my head, so I decided to write this book as a means of sharing what has worked for me along the way. I am offering it not as 'the ultimate bible of self-help', but as a bank of resources you can use to help you.

You might read this book from cover to cover and do all the exercises in order, or perhaps you will dip in and out. It is up to you to find what works best. It makes logical sense to read it all, but if during reading you think, 'no, this bit isn't for me', skip it, move on. If I thought I was writing a one-size-fits-all book, I would need my head examining. We are all completely different, but this stuff works, and I know it does; I have worked with, been friends with, coached and taught people just like you for decades and I test it all out daily. I know it will work for you because you will draw on what you need at the time that you need it.

Consider it a mini self-help library in one place, but not the be all and end all of libraries; it's the book you read, use and then go off and find out more from other people, websites and books. By reading this book you will have your own questions and thoughts, and perhaps the book will not answer all that you need to know – in fact I suspect it won't, and it shouldn't. There are lots of experts out there who will share their knowledge. Go find them. These pages contain decades of tried and tested methods, suggestions, exercises and things you might benefit from knowing about. If this book helps just one person have a better life, then I will feel that warm glow until the end of my days and the book will be a success.

As Seneca stated: 'As long as you live, keep learning how to live.'

Having read many self-help books, listened to hours upon hours of fabulous podcasts, attended courses and workshops and trained to become a life coach; I now know that if you actually want to get anything out of the self-help experience, you need to do some work. On yourself to start with. Identifying what you need to let go of is a pretty good place to start. I was born at a time where pen and paper was the means of journaling, and I still do to this day, it's a good habit to get into as it has been proven to release thoughts and start to enable you to process what's going on, even stuff from the subconscious mind comes out in journaling. It's also been demonstrated that using pen and paper aids the memory to engage in a way that typing into an electronic device does not. I highly recommend that you have a dedicated pad (and fancy pen too, if you like) to use as this book will give you numerous opportunities to write stuff out. (I have added 'notes' pages at the back of the book for those of you holding the printed version).

It has taken me over thirty years of being interested in the self-help world, lots of personal coaching, a bit of counselling, but mostly self-help books, podcasts, studying and journaling to get my head in a place where I genuinely have the relationships I want, with the people who matter and you can have that too. Those that are close to us, whether they are family members or friends, they know a lot about us and, therefore, when they let us down in some way, it hurts all the more because they are close, and so trusted. I had tended to view my life as one where I just wasn't very lucky with some people who were in it, but I see this differently now. I really think that they were lessons to be learned. I will share my process of letting go as it has simply saved my sanity. I look around my close family and friendship circle and think, it's true – you can choose who to have in your life, you are allowed to do this, so those who are close to me, family and friends alike, are the 'family' I have chosen for myself. And I have chosen very well.

I have personally failed more than I have succeeded, I have given up more than persevered. I am a work in progress, and you are too. I read those self-help books for a reason: they all gave me hope, I thought I would be fixed after reading each and every one. I saw a solution was promised, and perhaps I didn't do the work necessary, say the affirmations as much as I should, but I took something away from all of them. This book will share some ideas, some exercises and some hope that you can work on you, fix the bits that you need to fix and benefit from the experience of one who has tried, mucked it up a bit but is getting there. I do not promise a finished result, surely, if a self-help book 'works' you would read one, be 'fixed' and not need to read another.

I propose that we are changing minute by minute, hour by hour, growing and developing, reacting to our circumstances and, therefore, we are evolving all the time. It makes sense that what worked a decade ago, last month or yesterday might not be what you need right now. Where I quote a book or author I will detail their publications and websites, and I wholly advocate seeing what they offer, as it might suit you down to the ground.

What you can expect from reading

I promise not to overload you with exercises, but if you want to work on you, stopping for some self-reflection and a bit of work will help you move forward faster than skipping them altogether. I shall indicate places in the book where you might want to pause, do some journaling, check out a link or focus on an exercise. What you want to get out of this book, I trust you shall. It's up to you. I found out by reading book one, you need to do some reflection, navel gazing or sorting through your thoughts, and it does help – I promise. And it's likely to be a bit emotional, and we need to work with that – a key phrase I use to this day is *this too shall pass.* Because you know what? It really, really does.

You can work your way through this at your own leisure. I suspect it won't take you anywhere near thirty years to make the changes you need, because it doesn't have to. I will detail the things that slowed me down, and that got in my way, actually *I* got in my way, often. One thing to note is that the questions I ask of you will challenge you – how deep you go with your answers is up to you. The deeper you go, the more self-awareness and learning you shall receive. But if you are not ready, then just go as far as you feel you want to. The purpose of questions in this book is to get you to open up and face your truths, reveal stuff you have not thought about before and to make you aware of ways to deal with this stuff that has come up, it's not intended to scare the pants off you. So, work at your pace, but as I cover in chapter twelve – the real learning comes when you are out of your comfort zone. I encourage you to be brave, but work within parameters you set yourself, if a question simply gives you nothing, don't worry about it, move on to another.

The first thing I learned to do was forgive, and throughout I will share my experience as it is a) real life stuff, not made up and b) you have something to benchmark against, which may or may not be useful for you. (If it isn't, then feel free to skip.) This book is the way I want to use my life coaching and teaching experience, my love for self-improvement, the way I approached it and the wisdom of all those self-help books, podcasts and workshops. It's my way of giving back, as I appreciate that despite a lot of rubbish, I am most fortunate to have had this life so far and its experiences, I trust you can benefit in some way that suits you. Happy reading and thanks for picking the book up in the first place.

With love and luck for your journey to come – Jo, July 2021

PS. There is a notes section at the end for you to pop your answers onto, or use a journal/notepad, I do recommend handwriting as you work through the exercises.

PPS. Throughout the book, I have added links to the books I mention, these links are affiliated to Amazon and any commission I receive goes towards the upkeep of the website www.weareallaworkinprogress.co.uk

As mentioned in my introduction, the book by Marianne Power, *Help Me! One woman's quest to find out if self-help really can change her life* https://amzn.to/3wDA0xX

CHAPTER ONE

Failure to prepare is to prepare to fail

On a training course in 1989 (way before I had even heard the term 'self-help') the teachers who were preparing us, the first-year holiday reps, to go off to resorts dotted around the Mediterranean spoke of this thing called 'transactional analysis'. Transactional analysis, or TA to use the abbreviated term, is a theory devised by Eric Berne in the 1950s which covers the premise that we communicate using three ego states – parent, adult and child. We might use all three ego states at different times during one conversation, one hour or throughout the day, and this can depend on who we are with and how we are feeling. None of the stages are age-related. They are within each and every one of us, regardless of how long we have been on the planet.

Bear in mind that communication is not only the words that we use. Research shows that the words that we use in conversation count for only seven per cent of overall communication. Our body language makes up the majority, fifty-five per cent, of how we convey our message, and thirty-eight per cent is down to the tone of voice. So be mindful of your tone: if you feel sarcastic and, therefore, sound sarcastic, it doesn't matter how nice the chosen words are, you'll be perceived as sarcastic.

Let's look at each ego state a little closer so you can build an idea of what they might look and sound like; you may identify with each. Someone who is very like a specific ego state might spring to mind too, this is good as it means you can identify that you either have these ego states or have seen them in others, recognising them is part of the way to improve our interactions as I will go on to explain. An ego state affects not only your communication but your behaviour. I have created the following three descriptions from what I have seen whilst in the workplace, whilst coaching, when interacting with friends and family and in the classroom where I worked as a business lecturer.

An **adult** state might describe someone who sees things from both perspectives, is quite rational and non-judgemental, stays focused and present, and wants the best outcome for all. They want to understand who they are talking to, so they listen carefully, probably ask questions to check understanding, obtain all sides of the story and are good at creating solutions and knowing how to suggest them. A person who uses adult state communication is able to diffuse a situation and they tend to react in a calm manner and want an opportunity to fix things if there is turmoil. In general, they are easy to get along or work with.

Being in a **parent** state has nothing to do with age or actually being one yourself. When you are in parent state your words and actions are likely to be advisory or telling, for example you might take charge of a situation quite assertively. Parent state can be wonderful for getting things under control, for laying out the rules and ensuring everyone knows who is in charge. Someone who communicates using parent state might also be critical, perhaps not listen as well as they could and, at times, think they have all the answers. Deep down they want the absolute best for people, but may have their own agenda quite firmly in mind and can appear inflexible. Their intent is on safety which is a positive, but how they go about it can feel rigid and, therefore, negative. In the workplace and in life, this ego state can be too inflexible for some. We will go on to look at why this is later in the chapter.

In the **child** ego state, people can seem carefree, not at all bound by rules, and display a determination to have things go the way they want, at times regardless of the consequences. Child state can be tricky to handle as the person might refuse to carry out things expected of them, they might rebel against the rules and cause upset. Child state is the most free and loose of the states – spontaneous, imaginative and wanting to challenge the status quo. You might get a tantrum or two along the way if they are determined to do what they want rather than what's needed or when it comes to conforming to rules. Their strengths are in their ability to think creatively and come up with ideas that are not the norm.

In terms of an all-round communication and behaviour model, you can probably see that the preferred ego state to adopt is the **adult** one. In this state you are calm and collected, you allow others to behave as they wish, you are non-judgemental, understanding, wise, a great listener, empathetic, caring, assertive and able to see things from another's perspective. Quite a big ask of anyone, but this is the preferred state or mode in which to operate. The **parent** state has many good qualities, and some that are not so great. Likewise, the **child** state, so adopt the adult state as much as you are able.

When it comes to the communication between the states, the suggestion is that the adult (as the ideal state) converses with someone else, and regardless of age, this other person could be in child or parent state. The idea is that the adult stays adult and tries to get the person they are communicating with to change their style to adult. You can think of it as the adult encouraging their behaviour to breed behaviour, or that they are setting a good example. Just to be clear, the adult does their best to stay in adult, as it is the best communication state to adopt. I will give examples to help you grasp this concept if it is new to you.

Something else to remember is that if you are the person in child state (perhaps the child who is having a bit of a temper tantrum) you might trigger the other person's parent, or in other words bring out the parent in them. Likewise, if you are in parent mode and come across as being a bit bossy or condescending – you might trigger the child in the other person. As promised I shall give you some basic examples. Being triggered is so annoying yet such an easy thing to happen. As promised, here are some examples, in each one I have pointed out the trigger and where the adult remains adult. This all takes practice, but in my opinion it is a skill worth mastering.

A dialogue might go something like this:

> *Adult to adult*: I wondered if you might have that report for me?
> *Response is child*: I can't believe you expected me to be able to get that to you today!
> *Adult stays in adult*: Is there something I can help with so that it can be done today?
> *Child is now triggered into adult state*: Well, I could use a bit of help, thanks.

On the other hand, if the first adult had been triggered and slipped into parent state it could have gone like this:

> *Adult:* I wondered if you might have that report for me?
> *Response is child*: I can't believe you expected me to be able to get that to you today!
> *Adult now triggered into parent*: I do not like the tone of your voice, you have had ample time to do this!
> *Child remains*: You set an unreasonable deadline! My God, you always do this, expect us to provide work with unachievable deadlines.

We now have two people arguing, they refuse to speak or work together and the boss gets involved. It was so easily avoided by the adult staying in adult as in the first example.

Let's look at another case:

> *Adult*: You know what, I have had enough to drink, I think I am going to call it a night.

Response is parent: Oh, can't handle it, eh? Can't keep up with the rest of us, you need to stay and practise your drinking!
Adult remaining in adult: Not tonight, I am sure you'll all have a great time with or without me, I'm just going to do the rounds and say goodbye.
Parent triggered into adult: That's a shame. Can we catch up soon? I feel I've not really caught up with you.
Adult: Of course, I am free tomorrow, text me when you are up and about and let's do lunch!

I can feel the love, can you? But it could have gone like this:

Adult: You know what, I have had enough to drink, I think I am going to call it a night.
Response is parent: Oh, can't handle it, eh? Can't keep up with the rest of us, you need to stay and practise your drinking!
Adult triggered to child: I don't want to! I said I've had enough, you always try to get me to drink too much. I am just bored with you all repeating yourselves, you've all become annoying and I want to go home!
Parent: Oh, excuse me for breathing! You just don't know how to have fun; you've become so boring since you cut down on drink.
Adult still triggered to child: And you lot are a pain, always wanting to go out and spend loads on stupid overpriced cocktails to cheer up your boring lives, I can't even hear what's being said it's so loud in here.
And so on ... not feeling the love now, are we?

I have given you a basic overview and real-life examples of some excellent and really worthwhile research by Berne. Please, if the premise resonates with you, look at the links I have added below and find out more. There are many people out there training others in TA and I am a major fan. I am not saying I always stay in adult; I am human, and I get triggered just like the rest of us. When I teach teenagers, I always try to cover TA in the first term.

It is a wonderful tool to have use of when addressing a stroppy teenager. I once had one who was applying make-up in my lesson (yes this really happened, and I teach business not hair and beauty) I didn't actually need to do much as the exchange shows:

> *Me as adult*: Please can I ask you to put that away, thanks.
> *Student as child*: Nah, you're alright, Miss, I need to finish my eyebrows.
> *Me still as adult*: I can't start the lesson until that's all been put away, I need you to focus on the lesson and join in.
> *Student still as child*: Leave me alone, Miss, I can listen and do this.
> *Another student adopting parent*: You are behaving like a child, just do what she says.

What a beautiful moment. I didn't have to resort to anything else. It was always, of course, more effective when they were told by their peers, and I shall always be grateful to those in my classes that 'got' TA. It raised their game, they behaved better, they took responsibility and it made them a damn sight nicer to be around. In terms of their life skills, they were my 'distinction' students and I loved them for it. As I have indicated in the example, the second student went into parent mode, as that's what the first 'child' student had triggered in them. This could result in an argument, on this occasion the student with the make-up did tell them to shut up, the whole class was watching for the reaction, to see what would happen. I stayed silent – waiting – and the first student decided to capitulate and put her make-up away. It could have gone another way and quite honestly, I would have had to resort to parent. My class, my rules: make-up away or leave, basically. You can't let a whole class wait for a lesson because of one person putting on make-up, when let's face it – that's a pre-college activity.

Now we have arrived at the section of the book where you do your first exercise. Grab that pen and pad and consider these questions, it's useful to dig deep and be honest. I always keep my answers private, and if you are concerned that someone else might judge you for your honesty, you might elect to do this too. In my experience the real truth about your situation will be far more useful for you, I promise.

- Thinking of the three ego states – child, parent and adult – which is the one you think you use the most?
- Can you give examples?
- Why do you think that is the state you adopt most frequently?
- What does being in that state help you with?
- When is it not so useful?
- When have you noticed that you get triggered into other states?
- Are there certain people or situations that trigger you?
- Can you write out a quick dialogue of how this usually goes?

- Can you think of a way to stay in adult at these times?

- What will help you stay in adult overall?

Congratulations on doing that. Did it flag anything up that you need to work on? Anything to think about a bit more? Or are you one of the wonderful creatures that sail through life in adult at all times? If so, I want to be you. I am working on my adult daily. She is in there, it's just my child and parent can be noisy and unwelcome and I am aware that I need to improve staying in my adult state. Wherever you are right now, keep on working on your adult – as you can see from the examples and your answers to the questions, it will be hugely beneficial, improve your communication skills and help interactions, especially if you have a lot of people and/or situations which seem intent on triggering you out of adult.

If you wish, you could pause and take a look at the links I have given to information about TA online in the footnotes.[1] I haven't included anything from Wikipedia. As one used to teaching, I have had to explain to students that anyone can write Wiki and it's best to place ourselves in the hands of experts. Having said that, Wiki usually gives a very easy to understand explanation so can be a useful place to start.

Why we react to people in the way that we do is a complex and vast subject matter, and one that interests me immensely. We spend so much time interacting with others, from those we live with, to those we see out and about on an informal basis – on buses, in shops, at the hairdressers. All the time we are working with others, socialising and communicating with friends we are

---

[1] mcpt.co.uk/transactional-analysis-explained/affinitycentre.co.uk/transactional-analysis-theory-explained/

being ourselves and demonstrating who we are. If you are anything like me, you want to present the best version of yourself and so it's good to have an understanding of what's making us behave the way that we do, or to use another phrase – what makes us tick.

There's a book by Steve Peters called *The Chimp Paradox.* I actually asked my mum for this for Christmas during my second year of teaching teenagers. Why did I give up a bath set of gorgeous bubbles for a work-related book? Because teaching teenagers pushed my buttons like never before. At first, I didn't stop to realise that I was being triggered and could use my knowledge of TA to deal with it. I wanted to be able to understand a bit more about the way brains and the ego worked. I loved the book because the basic premise is that we all have a brain that's forged from our need to survive. So the 'chimp' part of the brain is the section that is 'hard wired', the part of the brain that can dig its heels in about stuff, be very inflexible, and push to win.

Obviously there is a lot more to be learned from reading the entire book. I recommend borrowing it from the library, or invest in a copy if this is an area you feel you need to explore more. If you are not massively competitive (like me) you might feel, you can override this need to win and ignore the chimp (and I believe that you can, to a certain extent, but it takes a lot of work) but once you are made aware, and let's face it, that's all that self-help does, it makes you aware of ways and techniques to handle what's going on for you. That's why you don't ever need just the one self-help book. You evolve, you change, you develop and morph each and every minute, even if you don't notice it. So at some point in your life, you might need 'book a' or 'seminar b' or 'workshop c', and that serves you at that precise moment in time – but then stuff comes up, usually from being an active participant in dealing with your life, and you might need or want to look at another aspect that's arisen for you.

When running my coaching business I preferred to look at how the ego (chimp) showed up as a two-part entity, the negative 'gremlin' and the positive 'cheerleader' or 'angel'. Depending on the client, we would use either term, as some found cheerleader 'too American'. Others thought angels too religious, at times we would have to create a totally new name. Gremlins however seemed to work for all. Perhaps you have seen that old film about the once cute but then demonic green goblin-type creatures sharing the same name? Well the gremlin is inside our head constantly and it's a chatty little bugger. It's the one we all hear, and it takes work to control it. Some call it 'negative self-talk', and it's loud, vocal and can stop you from doing all sorts of things.

As Henry Ford so aptly said: 'Whether you think you can or you think you can't, you're right.' When we allow the gremlin to dominate our thoughts, we think we can't. The gremlin is a genius in sabotage, and because the voice is inside your head, you mistake it for your actual thoughts, as Eckhart Tolle covers so beautifully in *The Power of Now*. Tolle suggests that we have the ability to listen to our own self-talk and be detached from it. What a great idea! Cut loose from this negative rubbish that the gremlin is spouting. But how? That's where practice makes perfect. But how to practise this? I shall share what has worked for me and for people I have worked with.

The books and their links are:
Steve Peters, The Chimp Paradox https://amzn.to/3hrNMPG
Eckhart Tolle, The Power of Now https://amzn.to/3e3iw7o

CHAPTER TWO

When I accidentally meet the 'Queen Bee' of British life coaching in a service station in Wales

Perhaps you have been there too? You are in a service station somewhere on a motorway, there is a loo stop planned and you hit the shop to stock up on water, cans of drink, chocolate and magazines for the journey and holiday ahead. We were a female-only group heading away to a mate's barn in the middle of nowhere in the Welsh countryside. The weather was due to be typically Welsh – rainy – so I grabbed my favourite of the time, *Marie Claire* and the first edition of *Glamour*. It had Kate Winslet on the cover as I recall and I probably did buy it for the cover story of Kate to be honest, but as it was likely to be handed round, I certainly wasn't that attached to it. *Glamour* was clearly American in its origins. I merely scanned it, as you do on holiday, as we had booze and fags and hours of drunken chats and backgammon to accommodate and I didn't really think much more of it.

It was only when I took the magazine home and could give it my undivided attention that I read an article on Fiona Harrold and her book *Be Your Own Life Coach*. The strapline promised that you could 'take control of your life and achieve your wildest dreams'. Me back in 2001 was desperate to take control of my life. Sod the wildest dreams bit. Just getting out of the mess I was in would have suited me. My relationship with alcohol was very unhealthy at this time. I indulged in wine every night and each weekend was just a blur of clubbing, dancing and chill-outs followed by weekdays at work, barely managing to get through until it all began again on Friday night.

I decided to buy Harrold's book and headed to Waterstones in Brighton to grab a copy. It was the beginning of a relationship with myself that I had no idea I needed. Firstly, I didn't realise how much writing I would want and need to do. Fortunately I am a keen diary keeper so this didn't pose an issue for me, but if this is an area you find challenging, I would say just try it, it can be very cathartic. Getting down on paper all that's in your head can give you sparks of connection to other aspects to look into more closely. I remember sitting on the bus to work each morning with a pad and pen balanced on my knee whilst I pondered each set of exercises. I amazed myself at how diligently I worked though the book.

It took weeks of soul searching and scribbling to finish it. The biggest realisations of all were around the area of forgiveness and letting go of past hurt and resentment. I am not going to lie, this was tough. I have a complicated relationship with some members of my family and from an early age was catapulted from living with my birth mother and siblings to being displaced to a half-sister's father and his new wife and young family. I refer to it as when I was adopted, but it was called guardianship back then – this was 1978 when I was eleven years of age. Whilst working through *Be Your Own Life Coach* in my twenties, I was suddenly faced with memories of things long ago that I quite clearly had not dealt with.

I am forever grateful to Fiona Harrold for writing that book, and also to myself for picking the magazine up in WHSmith, and for my tenacity in working through what was some quite painful stuff. Looking back, the alcohol reliance makes total sense, I can see that rather than sitting and examining past hurt, I was quite happy to numb myself. In fact, I remember thinking each night as I opened that bottle that in a little while I would not be 'thinking' anymore.

Instead of getting to grips with everything in my head – I was blocking it. I am aware that this is a reaction that I think most of us can identify with. You may not use bottles of Chardonnay, it may be other means that distract you – reality TV? Gossip magazines? Over exercising? Endless cleaning? Excessive eating? Shopping? What is that thing you do that means you don't have to think?

So, here comes your next exercise, try to answer the following as thoroughly and honestly as you can.

- What are you using to block out your thoughts?

- Why do you think you do that?

- Are there other ways that you avoid dealing with your thoughts?

- What is the benefit to you in having these other methods?

- What would be the benefit in stopping the blocking of your thoughts?

- Can you list three ideas or ways to stop?

- When will you stop?

- On a scale of zero to ten, ten being high, how motivated are you to stop?

In coaching terms, if you have written anything over a seven, it's a strong goal. Under seven, ask yourself, what can you do to strengthen your resolve to that goal?

Well done for giving your time and focus to that, if you discovered something interesting, or monumental or just a little bit curious, that's great. We all block thoughts, we all distract ourselves, one of my favourite sayings is that 'we get in our own way'. This saying is crystal clear to me, we stop the good stuff happening. We self-sabotage and it's useful to stop and understand why that might be and how we can change.

Personally, I was so affected by the self-coaching that I had just undertaken that I decided to leave my job that I didn't like all that much and start my own business. I just didn't know what in. All the exercises in the book had shown me how to take a hard look at what was in my own way. Most of it was my 'limiting self-belief'. I had never heard of this term before, but I was staggered to learn that I, a pretty upbeat, positive, gregarious and outgoing person, was actually walking around with a whole load of ideas about myself that were in direct opposition to the way I presented myself to the world. Anyone meeting me would recall a fun, chatty and confident person; I, on the other hand, now knew the truth. I presented that persona but didn't actually feel it. Working on your self-limiting beliefs is one of the most worthwhile things you can do. If you have many, like I do, then it might take some time. But it will be time worth spending.

How do we work out what they are? I found that mine came out when working on various coaching exercises. Looking at what you feel *you can't do* is a good starting point, so let's get you working on yours now. As I said, it'll be time well spent.

- What do you think you can't do?
- Why do you think this?
- What do you feel is beyond you?
- Why do you think this?
- What have you been told you can't do and by who?
- Do you agree/disagree? Why?
- Why might this person have said this?
- What would you love to do but have told yourself you can't?
- Why do you want to do this thing?
- How could you make it happen?

Hopefully, as you look over your answers, you will see where you are creating *I can't do* thoughts. If they are harmless in their context, then we can notice them but just let them go. If they are holding you back, and you feel they are true and it's stopping you from doing or being what you want, then they are self-limiting beliefs. To put it another way, you have identified a belief that you hold about yourself that is in your way. Keep a note of these below as we will work on them together.

My self-limiting beliefs are:

Now for each one (and as I indicated earlier, I had loads so don't worry if you do too, I think it's quite normal) you will write down *why* you think you hold this belief. Try to get into as much detail as you can, even if it sounds silly, in fact especially if it sounds silly. Some of my best lightbulb moments were when I was journaling and being playful about something and it hit a nerve instead. Basically, I was putting on an 'it's not important that they said or did this' act to myself, in private. But it did matter, because it hurt. Just write as much as you can, don't edit, let the thoughts come, pick over them afterwards.

The reason I hold these limiting self-beliefs are:

For the next questions, really go to town, think in as much detail as you can, be specific, they are designed to get you to list what your ideal life or dream is.

> Where would you like to be in ten years' time? Think geographically, career-wise, relationships, family, friends, home, health and fitness, hobbies, money, travel, spiritual journey, and anything else that's relevant to you.

> Where would you like to be in five years? Think geographically, career-wise, relationships, family, friends, home, health and fitness, hobbies, money, travel, spiritual journey, and anything else that's relevant to you.

> Where would you like to be in one year? Think geographically, career-wise, relationships, family, friends, home, health and fitness, hobbies, money, travel, spiritual journey, and anything else that's relevant to you.

Notice that the exercise started with the furthest timeline. This is deliberate in order to get you to think of your ideal life or your dream, then as you set the closer deadlines you might notice that you state goals to help attain the longer-term objective. If this isn't how yours look, please do not worry, there is no right or wrong when it comes to your own dreams. If what you want makes sense to you and you feel motivated and compelled to make it happen, then why should I or anyone else tell you that you can't, shouldn't, or that you are being unrealistic?

When I have set myself a goal, I like to write it down, set reminders, use sticky notes and generally keep the goal somewhere visual as a prompt. I might also have a set time of the day or week to work on that target. Because a goal is just an idea, until you take action. Do I share my ambitions? Only with carefully trusted people. I have learned the hard way about this one. Over the years, I have had a couple of long-standing friends who seemed intent on making negative remarks when I am casually chatting about things I am doing, trying to do or even thinking of doing. I now recognise them for what they are: displays of their own discomfort.

I like a quote by Wayne Dyer: 'How people treat you is their karma; how you react is yours.' Or as I used to say, 'it's their shit not mine'. Without psychoanalysing my pals, they don't think as I do, they don't share a lot of my values and beliefs and, therefore, when I open my mouth and start getting all excited about this month's new project, they are nowhere near the same page as me. They do not get it. And that's OK. You and I are not writing out what *they* want, we are setting down what *we* want. You might find that you decide not to share your ideas and dreams with others because, like me, you are wary of their reaction. It could demotivate you if you are harbouring self-limiting beliefs or even straightforward doubts.

Here are some of the less useful comments I have had in my time:

'I can't see that working out.'
'It takes a long time to get published, you know.'
'I am sure you'll give up, you usually do.'
'You are thinking beyond your means. Who do you think you are? You'll never pull that off.'
'Don't you think it'd be better to get a nice job/get married/pay off the mortgage?'
'There are no jobs in that sector at the moment.'

There are more to add to this list, perhaps you've had your array of unhelpful comments too? It's worth taking a few minutes to note them. Get them out of your head and onto paper. You could even write them out and set fire to them. Just be careful where you do this.

The reason I brought these up is that over the years they have stopped me – let me rephrase that – I have allowed these sorts of comments to stop me. If the person delivering this opinion is someone you rarely see or don't really like, then it will probably wash over you. The statements above were made by those close to me and they caused me to feel less confident, less capable, less likely to do what it was that I wanted to do. I have worked on myself continually since 2001 and I can announce that the people with these negative remarks are no longer in my inner circle. I happily removed them. Because their comments really do say more about them than me.

Another thing you can do, which is so simple and so effective, is to use affirmations. One of the earliest things I ever came across was the idea that if the subconscious mind files things as fact, then we might as well feed it well: with positive affirmations. The only thing to remember about these is that they must be present tense and personal. They need to start with: 'I am' or 'I have' and go on to state something positive. You are not helping yourself if you say to yourself: 'I must lose weight'. You can change this to: 'I am loving my new diet', 'I have a great body' or 'I am enjoying exercise'. Play around with some that address areas you are not happy with, and feed that subconscious mind with healthy, positive thoughts. It will change how you feel, perhaps not immediately, but over time. It is best to repeat affirmations, either out loud or in your head, over and over again. If, like me, you start off by feeling a bit silly and self-conscious, that's OK, they are only in your head, no one needs to know what you are feeding your subconscious with. Just like no one needs to know you are doing pelvic floor exercises, some things can stay private.

If you start to notice that you are feeling better, more positive and generally happier after doing affirmations, then I would encourage you to carry on. The majority of people I have advised to try them have reported that they felt better for doing so, so for the sake of a few minutes of repetition, they can really benefit.

Let's take a few minutes here to get you to list some affirmations that will help you feel better about yourself – why not try to come up with ten?

I am ...
I am ...
I am ...
I am ...
I am ...
I have ...
I have ...
I have ...
I have ...
I have ...

Don't worry if you are a bit short of ten, however many you have, as long as they feel right for you, is the right number. Now try saying them over and over and see if they make you feel better. I love affirmations, they're one of the easiest ways to nudge great thoughts into the subconscious which can be a rather gremlin-dominated place.

When you are proud of a goal, an idea or a dream – whether it's running Couch to 5K, losing weight, making your own dress for your wedding or launching a business – you can be fizzing with excitement. You have seen a thing you are convinced you can do and you have the passion, desire and motivation to do it. So of course, you pop onto your social media channel and announce it to your best pals and family, and then if you are unlucky enough to have negative ninnies in your life, and I think we all do, the remarks will start. They might be prefaced with, 'I am saying this for your own good ...' or, 'Darling, you should hear it from me, everyone thinks that ...' or some such introduction.

It took me years to detach from any of these remarks, literally two decades or so of work. I hope it doesn't take you anywhere near that timeframe (I am convinced I am a slow learner in matters of self-protection, you don't have to be) The first thing is to hear what's being said and note that it's a) Not positive (should be easy to spot!) and b) What is their fear? Yes, *their* fear. Because they are being triggered by what you are doing, if they weren't *they wouldn't pass comment*. Let's take the above examples and I will share with you *their* fear as I can recall the person, time and place of each remark.

'I can't see that working out,' translates to, 'I couldn't do it.' Their fear is their lack of ability. *Not yours.*

'It takes a long time to get published, you know,' was actually, 'I am not patient and could never wait.' Their fear is that they don't give things enough time. *Not yours.*

'You'll never pull that off. I am sure you'll give up, you usually do,' becomes, 'I do not stick at anything new and I am scared to try.' A clear fear of theirs. *Not yours.*

'Don't you think it'd be better to get a nice job/get married/pay off the mortgage,' is them saying, 'I am stuck, I have no freedom.' Their big fear is that they wasted their time. *Not yours.*

'There are no jobs in that sector at the moment,' suggests that they are afraid that they are stuck in some way (probably workwise) and you should be too. Again, *not yours*.

All of the above, are my take on that person's comment, if we asked them I am ninety-nine per cent sure they would deny my suggestion and say they were only trying to help me. I actually think it's more likely that they were projecting their fear on to me. If someone isn't in a great place themselves we may not know it, but if they project something onto us then it's quite a clear indicator that something is going on. At this stage, you have a choice. You can use what you've heard to ask questions and check in on them. In my experience, their fears pop out in conversation and the delivery of their statements can be from their subconscious mind – they are not even aware it's a fear of theirs. In which case, you might be trying to open up a conversation about an anxiety that person has not even acknowledged is there.

For now, it might be an idea to just listen out for people's fears and understand that they aren't deliberately trying to sabotage you, they think they are being helpful. If you have done your homework and researched your goal and how to achieve it, then you can stay assured that you have a good chance of success. And basically, let them get on with their own lives. I only mention this because I have fallen foul to a lot of it in the past, and at times it actually spurred me on, in a headstrong 'I'll show you' way. So it can actually work as a motivation, it's up to you how you use it. If certain people are constantly projecting and generally not being supportive, you might want to go elsewhere for positive encouragement.

Creating your ideal future is an important stage in working out what you want. You can of course, write it all down and not do anything about it. After all, it's your life, and it's always your choice. I would ask that you think about the consequences of not doing anything, as well as those of doing something. When I read over how I had planned my future ideal life, I knew that I had to give running a business a go. It felt right and I had very little to hold me back. I could work from home and I had a partner with whom I shared the bills and who was happy to support me, so I knew that I wouldn't become homeless if it failed. Basically, I wrote out all the pros and cons. The pluses, the minuses. I felt that if I at least did that, then I was as prepared for this new venture as I could be.

I was about to embark on a sharp learning curve that would catapult me into a world where I could make the rules, the hours and the money I needed to live on. Initially I thought, why isn't everyone doing this? After a year, I understood why. I had a business partner at first and we shared the workload, then she decided it wasn't for her. I think I was too busy to really stop and work on that one at the time, it certainly provided more stress and worry having to carry on without her. Trying to get a brand-new idea established, marketed and profitable, is actually really tough. I loved all the networking opportunities and meeting new people, I hated the book-keeping and endless admin.

I was determined – I knew that businesses take a few years to establish and I didn't want to give up without trying this, that or the other. I always had ideas and strategies to try out, and I had continued to review the coaching book, using exercises found within its covers to keep me motivated. I never really admitted it couldn't work, but at around the eight-month period I realised that the money wasn't there. I was using my savings up faster than projected, and the client base wasn't expanding. I did not want to stop, I knew I needed time, but cash flow is something you cannot ignore. It was at this time that I looked into becoming a life coach myself. This was 2002, life coaching was taking off in the UK. I wanted a qualification rather than to just read another book or attend a seminar. The coaching industry was unregulated but I could see that the amount of stuff that comes up when you take a good hard look at your life can be a little overwhelming, and I wanted to ensure I was doing this properly.

At the time the, now disbanded, United Kingdom College of Life Coaching (UKCLC) offered a course that was accredited by a University. I embarked on a one-year course to get the qualification. During the initial training I was introduced to the Wheel of Life and the TGROW (Topic, Goal, Reality, Options and Way forward) model for the first time. I will share these with you in this chapter, as they are easy to use and useful for self-coaching, even if you only have five or ten minutes to do a quick exercise.

On the course we had to coach one another in order to increase our hours of actual coaching, plus read numerous books to support the written modular work in order to complete the qualification. Due to running a business at the same time, it took me a bit longer than a year to get qualified but when I did achieve it in 2004 I knew I had another skill for life. I then diversified my company into two sections: I ran events, which utilised my organisational skills, and I also coached business owners in the media field. Everything went brilliantly for a while – then it didn't. I just couldn't get the clients and without their payments I needed to work part-time to support myself. I then had to give up and take a full-time job. It was hard to leave the business behind after three years of hard work and long hours, but I took the decision to close as it was no longer making me happy.

Looking back, getting the coaching qualification was one of the best things I ever did for myself. I chose to do it for business reasons, but I ended up rewarding myself with skills for life. The work that I had started by using Fiona Harrold's book was magnified and enhanced. In order to coach someone you need to take a good hard look at yourself and where you are at. By spending this precious time on myself I really got to grips with who I was, what motivated me, what stopped me and what I could do about all of it.

One of the most useful tools was the Wheel of Life and I still use it on a weekly basis, as you can quickly scribble out a circle and divide into eight sections (or into a pizza as a student I taught once called it) [2]

Wheel of Life

Name: ____________

Date: ____________

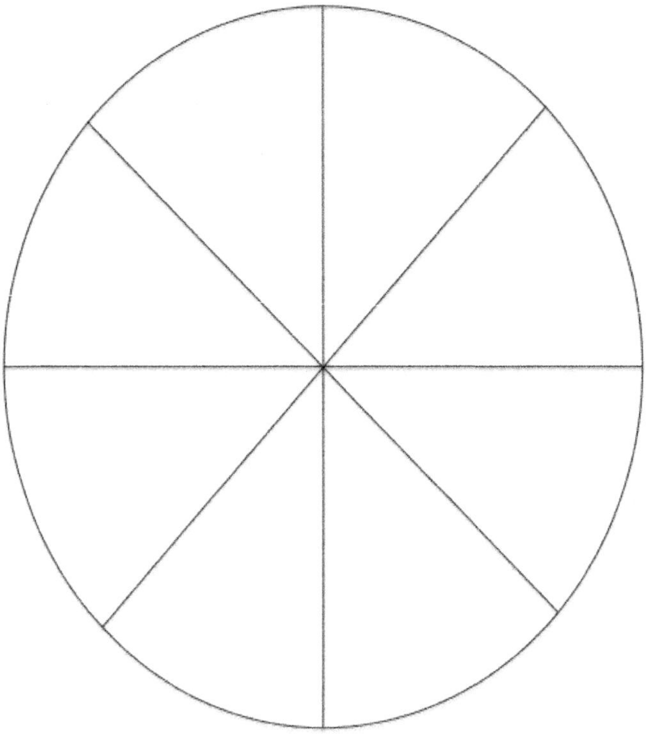

[2] There are many Wheel of Life templates online, thanks to raviraman.com for this simple one.

What you choose to name the different sections is up to you. The eight we used on the course, and I still use to this day are:

- Health
- Career
- Finances
- Significant other
- Friends and family
- Personal Growth
- Physical environment, for example home
- Spirituality

It's your wheel so feel free to tailor it to suit you best. Some other names for sections you could use are:

- Fun
- Fitness
- Hobbies
- Learning
- Travel
- Food or diet
- Business

Once you have named each section of the wheel, rate yourself out of ten in accordance with how happy you are in each section. Zero is the lowest and sits in the centre of the wheel; ten is on the outside edge. You rate each section then draw a line to join up the sections. Your perfect life is ten out of ten and that's depicted by the outside edge of the wheel. What you score inside shows you how wobbly your journey through life might be, if this was a wheel on a car or bicycle.

To follow are two examples that I located online. One has eight sections but if you are stuck and can only come up with seven use the latter for inspiration.

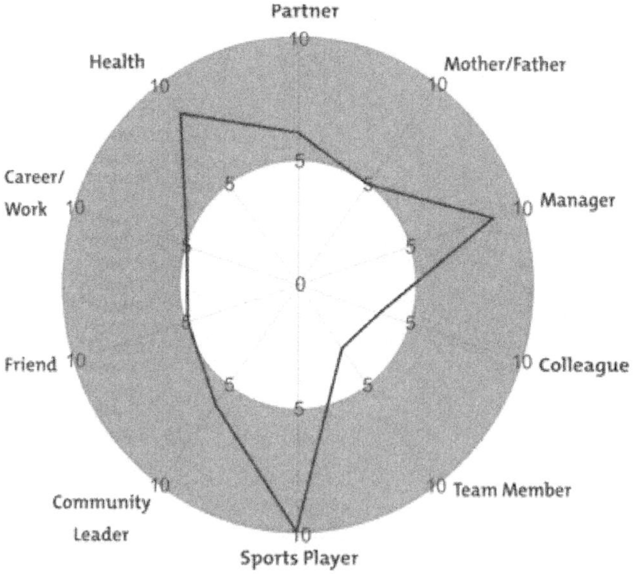

3

Here is a seven-section example.[4]

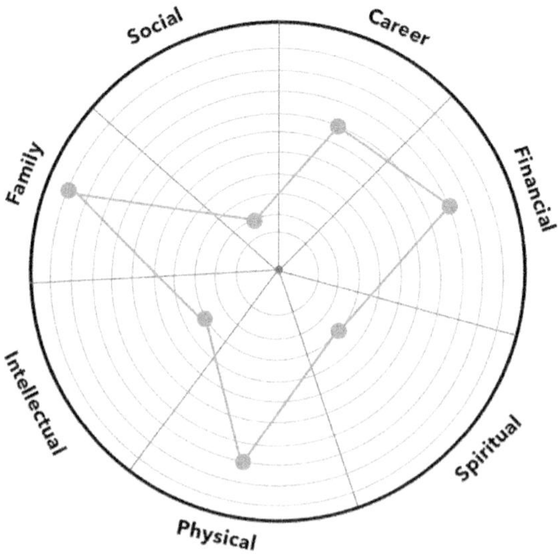

[3] https://www.mindtools.com/pages/article/newHTE_93.htm
[4] https://minimalism.co/articles/wheel-of-life

Please go ahead and complete a Wheel of Life: name your sections, then grade yourself where you are today. The more you do Wheel of Life exercises, the more the sections and their grades shift about. This is natural and to be expected. As I mentioned before, your life does not stay static, things do shift and when I scribble out a Wheel of Life on a weekly basis I often see sections and their grades go from one extreme to another. You work with what you have today. Don't worry too much about where you were, that's the past (unless comparing is useful to you). I tend to encourage focus on how to change the scoring in order to make each section better **today.** Each section represents an area of your life and how you are feeling, and making you happier and better each and every day is the purpose of this book and, therefore, this exercise.

Once you have numbered each section of your wheel, you can then see at a glance which areas of your life are most in need of work. As I mentioned previously, in coaching terms anything seven and above is pretty good, so I would focus on those below this. Now you have identified them, what do you do with them?

This is where TGROW comes in. The beauty of this model lies in the simple yet open questions you can ask yourself within each step of the model. Those of us wanting to know what is going on and why use open questions a lot. They are number one in a coach's toolkit and can benefit us in all walks of life.

Taking your lowest grades, identify your sections from the Wheel of Life that need the most work – for example if you rated money as two out of ten I think it's safe to say that section requires some work to get it to seven, which is where we would say it's in a pretty good place, and indeed we would plan to get it to ten out of ten in time.

Below are the prompts to use when completing a TGROW model.

> **Topic**: what you need to work on – give a simple explanation.
> **Goal**: it's best to make this SMART – specific, measurable, achievable, realistic and timed.

Reality: where you are now – what's going on for you – what's holding you here – your thoughts about where you are.

Opportunity: what could you do to change this – what options do you have – who might help – what do you need to make this happen – what little step could you take towards it today?

Way forward – when will you start on your goal – what is your motivation to do so on a scale of one to ten?

Now I shall give you an example from an actual Wheel of Life. In this instance, the section marked 'significant other' is a zero.

Topic: what you need to work on – give a simple explanation.

I would like to meet someone to be in a relationship with that leads to marriage.

Goal: it's best to make this SMART – specific, measurable, achievable, realistic and timed.

To attend different Meetup groups based in Northampton and the surrounding area on a weekly basis across a range of interests, such as walking groups, cycling groups, pub quizzes, gig trips and bar crawls. To research online dating options for my age group and level of intent (marriage as opposed to hook ups or casual relationships), starting today.

Reality: where you are now – what's going on for you – what's holding you here – your thoughts about where you are.

I am very happy being single, but it would be lovely to meet someone special to spend time with, go on holiday with, share my life with in the long term. Living in a city should provide ample opportunities to meet people, but I just do not go out. This needs to change. I get in from work, I am tired and can't be bothered. All my friends are in couples, and I am not meeting men through them. If I want to meet someone I need to make an effort and online dating has been awful, so it puts me off.

Opportunity: what could you do to change this – what options do you have – who might help – what do you need to make this happen – what little step could you take towards it today?
Not all online dating is the same, surely? I need to ask my friends what sites they met on and do some research to work out which might suit me. It feels like a numbers game, so the more people I meet surely the more chance I have of meeting someone. I liked the Meetup groups I have used in the past, so I need to try more of them, one new one per week. I could ask a friend to come with me if I think I am going to stay at home.
Way forward – when will you start on your goal – what is your motivation to do so on a scale of one to ten?
I will start researching Meetup groups and online dating for about an hour and see what looks good. I will contact two friends and ask if they will help me by coming along for moral support. I will do all of this today! My motivation to do so is eight out of ten.

If you get to 'Way forward' and your motivation grade is less than a seven, this might indicate that you don't really want to change this area of your life as much as you thought. You could redo the TGROW exercise and see how you could raise it to above seven. If that doesn't work, then you might need to admit it's not actually that important to you, or something else is in the way.

With the above example there is a telling line that the client writes in 'reality', did you spot it? *I am very happy being single.* If I was coaching this client and this came up, I might question them around this. Do they want to meet someone, or think they should? We live in a very couple-centric world, for a lot of people the journey from cradle to grave follows quite an exact path, but there are very happy single people all over the planet. Perhaps the client likes singledom but feels they are missing out? As I said, I would explore this a bit more. In coaching terms it could be a block. In the same stage, 'reality', the client also mentioned *online dating has been awful, so it puts me off.*

If this was my client or if this comes up in your exercise, it could be worth thinking of alternative options. Is there any point revisiting the online dating world if it has been so bad? 'What else could I do?' is a good question to move our thinking on to new options. Keep prodding at obvious blocks you have identified, not liking the online world and enjoying being single are, to my mind, potential blocks to the action the client has stated they will do. Fear of awful experiences can keep us on the sofa watching Netflix. Which brings me to examining how we can and do stop or block ourselves – it tends to be down to not wanting to leave our comfort zones.

To obtain a copy of Fiona Harrold's book: Be Your Own Life Coach I have a link for you to use here: https://amzn.to/3hSiH6L

CHAPTER THREE

'You must do the thing you think you cannot do'
– Eleanor Roosevelt

Being a life coach and running my own business working with clients was a dream come true for me, who would have thought that picking up a new magazine in a service station could lead to something so profound and wonderful? It just goes to show that you never know where your inspiration might come from. I remember being told on the coaching training course that as a dentist needs a dentist, a hairdresser needs a hairdresser, so a coach needs a coach. Part of the training was, as I mentioned, getting your practice hours done, so that when you were ready to coach paying clients you had a wide range of situations and experiences to draw upon. The number one thing that I always did with any person I coached, whether they were paying or I was practising, was to get them to look at their core values.

Values are, by definition: 'principles or standards of behaviour; one's judgement of what is important in life.' Whenever you start looking at your life and at the way you wish to work on it, change it, improve or develop it, I feel very strongly that in order to be successful, you need to understand your core values. Making decisions that support what's important in your life means that you are more likely to feel that you have made the right decision, be more committed and generally, find that it feels easier to make changes.

A values exercise can be very easy or quite complex depending on how in touch with your values you already are. There follows a list of some values for you to look over, you might need to add your own, but there should be no more than five core values. For them to be meaningful they need to be what you really feel, and not what you think society or somebody else thinks you should value. It's been said that you don't choose your values, they reveal themselves to you. I agree wholeheartedly. However, if you are totally stuck and don't know what is 'right', there are countless lists online for you to read over and choose based on your gut, heart or head reaction to them. In essence, you will know what feels right for you to choose as your values. I have included a list here for you to use and there is a link in the footnote to another site I think might benefit you.[5]

Dependability	**Balance**
Reliability	**Growth**
Loyalty	**Purpose**
Commitment	**Happiness**
Open-mindedness	**Health**
Consistency	**Honesty**
Efficiency	**Innovation**
Creativity	**Good humour**
Compassion	**Spirit of adventure**
Motivation	**Positivity**
Optimism	**Passion**
Respect	**Fitness**
Courage	**Education**
Perseverance	**Service to others**
Environmentalism	**Make a difference**

Are you able to choose a maximum of five from this list or using those in the link? Once you have the five written down, now put them in order of importance to you.

[5] https://scottjeffrey.com/core-values-list/

1.
2.
3.
4.
5.

Now you have these values and they are in order of importance, they can be used straight away. I would write them down where you will see them daily – a reminder on a phone, across your screensaver, sticky notes on the bathroom mirror or on your PC or laptop. Display them and get used to them as they will help you shape your decisions. When you set a goal or an intention, ask yourself – is this honouring my core values? If the answer is no, re-evaluate the goal or intention.

For example, health is my number two value. Despite knowing this I have been known to drink too much wine, eat too much cake, chocolate and biscuits and skip the gym because I wanted to go home and watch Netflix. I know, appalling behaviour. Whilst in the Covid-19 lockdown, I told myself that as the gym was closed and I would be home anyway, I might as well have nice treats to help me get through it. Then I asked myself if this was honouring my health value and of course, the answer was no. I revealed to a fitness friend that I was feeling lazy and slovenly and seemed incapable of working out at home. (Preferring tea, biscuits and a good book instead.) She immediately sent me loads of links to fun YouTube workouts she knew I would like.

When shopping I would pause with my hand over the carrot cake and have a quick core values conversation with myself. In my head, not out loud. I decided to skip alcohol for three months altogether, as I can drink alone with absolutely no qualms and again, I could see the period of enforced isolation becoming a steady decline into too much booze. Not immediately, but over a period of weeks rather than months, I got myself into a health-based routine that I stick to because the minute I cheat myself, I feel a bit silly. I know I don't really want to cheat, it's just that wine and carrot cake are really tasty and my willpower slips a bit.

I keep my eye on the goal I set: to stay the weight I am by the time lockdown ends. I guessed this would be three months, so my goal was specific – eat well, avoid certain foods, exercise twice a week, up my water intake, stay off the booze. It was measurable – I measure myself as I don't have weighing scales, and so far, I am the same dimensions. The goal was achievable, I wasn't suggesting I would end up a size ten, I wanted to remain a healthy size for me, which is size fourteen and I wanted to still fit in my clothes. It was realistic – I can leave the cake and Chardonnay in the shop. I can work out twice a week and remember to drink water. It was timed too. Plus it all aligned with and honoured my health which is my number two value. Was it easy? At times, no it wasn't. I dream of treats sometimes, but that's OK, I don't buy it and don't need it. I love Nairns oat biscuits instead, they fill me up, are low in sugar and come in super flavours including one with chocolate bits. I've also allowed myself some seventy per cent chocolate as it's high in antioxidants and tastes great too.

If you want anything enough, you will do the work. If you don't want it badly enough, you won't. As I have mentioned before – choose goals/intentions that really motivate you and you will make the changes you need. Maybe, like me, it won't be straight away, because we are human and we slip up and we fail. But if we want to change, we make it happen. What I will share with you at this stage is that I have noticed the priority of my values can change depending upon my personal circumstances. Ten years ago, I would not have had 'work–life balance' in my top five values. Right now, it is number one due to having been in a workplace that seems to have forgotten what the words mean. We can choose to shuffle the order and indeed add new ones, as our lives evolve and change.

CHAPTER FOUR

What if? Using the past to heal and help the present and the future

This book wasn't written as any sort of autobiography, and where I am sharing my life story from time to time it's in order to aid context and examples. I was once told, 'Write what you know.' It was good advice. I know what's gone before and I know, with the benefit of self-reflection, what has worked. I also know that it's a game of trial and error, this thing called life. No one can guarantee you an outcome or result, only you can work towards the one that you want. Using the past can be useful to identify what you feel was missed, and if it is still missing and that bothers you, you can choose to do something about it.

A timeline can be really useful as an exercise – if, to paraphrase Steve Jobs, we can only join the dots up looking backwards, then looking back might throw up some areas we are unhappy with and rather than accept that as a fait accompli, we can perhaps, take that past example and change it now.

One exercise you could do is to draw a horizontal line across some paper and write down key stages of your life, by age perhaps, or in any way that makes sense to you. You could add important events to this timeline. Or you can simply identify milestones and note them on a piece of paper. You could mind map this, using colour and images. There is no right or wrong way. Do what works for you. My preferred method was to simply note the areas where I felt I wasn't given the best opportunity and these examples include:

- Not attending school on a full-time basis until the age of eleven
- Being brought up around people freely using drugs and alcohol
- Separated from maternal mother and siblings at a young age
- Being bullied at the first school I attended full-time
- Lack of financial education

I would like to invite you to write yours down, they can be whatever you want them to be, and as many as you want.

So, now we have identified them, do we want to do anything about them? This is where TGROW can be used easily, just be aware that some will take a lot longer to work on in order for you to be happy with the outcome than others.

If we take a look at mine, I can let you know the time span and what actions I have taken:

- *Not attending school on a full-time basis until the age of eleven*
  I attended evening classes from the age of sixteen, attained a degree in my early forties, achieved a professional graduate qualification in my early fifties – lots of hard work and studying.

- *Being brought up around people freely using drugs and alcohol*
  Years of binge drinking ended up with me seeking professional help, and I read prolifically around the subject of alcohol and stopped drinking in my early fifties.

- *Separated from maternal mother and siblings at a young age*
  I would say this is resolved in as far as I have the relationships with the family members I feel 'get me', it has taken decades of work however – mainly around the subject of forgiveness.

- *Being bullied at the first school I attended full-time*
  By becoming a teacher, I was able to use my position to deal with those bullied and the bullies and work to prevent what happened to me happening to them – I can see that the negative experience made me stronger – I also used forgiveness techniques in this area too.
- *Lack of financial education*
  Taking personal responsibility has taken decades and I can truly say this is where I am very much a work in progress – I am attempting to make up for years of bad habits and where my pension and mortgage are concerned, all I can say is: I will get there!

By looking over my list, I can see that all these areas have been worked on, some a bit later than others (finances and drinking) but education and forgiveness have been ongoing for decades.

Please take some time to answer the following questions, it will be cathartic I am sure:

- Can you look over your list and see how far you have already come?

- Can you identify the ways you have changed in your life where these areas are concerned?

- What are the things you have identified that you are proud of?

- Where can you congratulate yourself?

- Where do you feel you need to do more?

Again, well done for being honest with yourself and getting this stuff out of your head and onto paper. What you choose to do with it, that's up to you. I hope you can use the tools already provided to help you if you decide that you want to do the work – but only when you are ready. Good luck!

CHAPTER FIVE

We are all in the gutter, but some of us are looking at the stars – Oscar Wilde

As I mentioned, when I did my life-coach training, we had to coach and be coached. I got a lot out of this on a personal level, working with others who wanted to encourage you to be the best version of yourself is a wonderful experience and I will always be very pro-coaching. As I will discuss, I have had counselling on a few occasions, and for me it really worked. In my experience, counselling involves taking time to look at the past. Perhaps I am scared of really addressing my history, so I have resisted looking back, and when I did I found it uncomfortable at times. When we leave our comfort zones there are growing pains to endure. As we stretch our discomfort it becomes comfort, so I understand the need to do so, and counselling will always have a place for me. But I have always got a lot out of the coaching relationships I have had over the years, whether it be from those 'trying it out on one another' trainee coach to trainee coach relationships, or from the professional coaches I have hired whilst running businesses or when faced with a crossroads in my life.

I find coaching is more focused on the future, at least the style I was trained in does. I am a non-directive coach, meaning I am not about to sit and wax lyrical about the most fabulous ideas that I have that will sort your stuff out right now. Non-directive coaching isn't about finding a solution for the person you are working with, it suggests that the person who seeks the coaching has all the answers. The coach is skilled and trained to encourage you, to tease out your answers and motivate you to get to where you want to go. Whenever I am stuck, I ask someone I trust who they worked with last and always go on personal recommendation.

One of the most fascinating areas I learned about in my training was to do with the subconscious and conscious mind. It was described to me that the conscious mind is the one that takes information and questions it. For example, you are asked to do a task at work, if you question in order to understand the full remit of the task, the deadline and check that you understand what is required, you are using the conscious mind. On the other hand, the subconscious mind is the part of the brain that simply files things as fact. When it hears a task, it logs that you need to do it. End of. Not how, by when, with whom, where it's needed, the why nor what it actually is. The subconscious can fuel the gremlin and our negative self-doubt because it files everything as fact. Someone told you your legs were fat in a miniskirt when you were fourteen? If the subconscious filed it away as fact, then you might believe you have fat legs and cover them up. This is what my subconscious did to me.

Whilst working on an exercise about how I viewed myself, I said that I believed I had fat legs. The person I was sharing this with looked stunned. They didn't see that. I thought they were being kind. But I started wearing more fitted trousers and jeans, shorter dresses and even miniskirts to test this out, and you've guessed it, it was noticeable that the majority of compliments I started to receive were about my 'great' legs. Who knew? I didn't, I had wasted years of covering up because of one remark that my subconscious recorded as fact. I remember exactly where it happened, who it was that said it, the tone of their voice, how it made me feel, I can even remember the offending article, a pale peach linen skirt, I can recall where I was going that night, and I remember spending all evening feeling awkward and self-consciously pulling my skirt down as much as I could. I was fourteen years of age and on a night out, I should have been dancing the night away and flirting with boys, but there you have it, a thoughtless comment from someone, filed as fact. When I found out years later that they were jealous and resented me, I could have kicked myself for taking it to heart. The subconscious has a lot to answer for. Include as much detail as you want when answering the following:

- Can you write down any harmful self-beliefs that you have about yourself, your personality or physical appearance?

- Can you trace them back to where they came from?

- Can you locate the cause of your way of thinking?

Now you have located this or these belief/s about yourself, I want you to write the opposite. For example, mine would change from, 'I hate my legs,' to, 'I have great legs.' Over to you:

I have great legs is an affirmation and, as we covered before, affirming this new positive statement can really help shift your thinking. It might take a bit more than just writing down a new affirmation, you might need to journal the heck out of it, talk to trusted people, or it might be that by tracing the cause of the belief you hold, you discover that it is so clearly false that you can move onto this new positive way of thinking easily.

This exercise can be useful for when our negative self-talk gets a bit busy. If your gremlin is having a chatty day, it's really worth noting what it says. If you can understand where the source of these remarks lie, you can work on them, reduce their impact by tracing and understanding the source. It might have been a comment meant to hurt you, or it might have been one that was meant to be funny. In my family, sarcasm and 'funny' retorts were all too common. I was a sensitive child and I know my subconscious logged a lot of it as fact, it's taken years to catch the sources, apply grown-up logic to it and reduce the thoughts and feelings I have about myself to a state where I can actually feel sorry for the person who delivered that retort.

They are in pain themselves, and that's what you end up on the receiving end of at times. Happy people don't try to make other people feel bad. Knowing that's what it is, can free you up to stop believing it and enable you to move on. Don't worry about them, unless you are trained in some way, I doubt you can help them. Work on yourself first, if you want to swing back and chat to them about their stuff, help them to work on themselves, you might be successful. In my experience, it is only people that are aware they need any help in the first place that are open to seeking it. A lot of people never acknowledge that they may need to sort their own issues out. As they say on airlines during the safety demonstration: put your own oxygen mask on first before helping others. You come first, work on you. Your good example might encourage others and if they come to you asking how you are getting your stuff together, growing and developing into a more amazing human being, you can help them then.

Forgiveness has been mentioned earlier. When I truly forgave those I felt had hurt me, I lost the anger and disappointment I had. This result was simply through accepting that it wasn't worth holding onto these feelings anymore. To this day, that is the one of the best and most meaningful gifts I could have given myself. My own personal gremlin likes to throw these 'failed relationships' in my face from time to time, usually upon waking up in the middle of the night.

I read somewhere that no good comes of the thinking we do between 11 p.m. and 7 a.m. therefore, I try to switch my brain off if I wake up between these times. This is where meditation comes in, and we are going to look at that in detail. When my gremlin chucks these 'failures' at me, my brain can't help but engage and off I go thinking about all the details, the 'who said what' and rehashing the whole episode over and over. There is never a different outcome, I always end up thinking that I made the right decision at the time and tell myself to let go of the 'conversation' that's really not worth having for the umpteenth time.

But have it over and over again, I do. I recently thought that perhaps a bout of counselling might be worth a go, I could try and work out why the recurring thoughts keep coming back, is this unresolved business I ask myself, am I truly happy with the outcome? If I am constantly thinking of certain people and the breakdown in our relationship, does this herald a need to review my decision and perhaps do something different?

This train of thought can go on for months, or in the case of one family member, years. To my conscious mind it appears to have been resolved, but there is no relationship so it is not really resolved. If the idea of counselling has appeared then is it the answer? I truly believe that counselling is an excellent way of working through things, counsellors are highly trained and specialised and if you are not reaching your own happy conclusion, then it might be worth a go. In my situation, it is damaged relationships that bother me the most, as I can't seem to accept that they have been broken and even though it felt like it was for the best at the time, perhaps I was wrong? We all make mistakes. The greatest learning can come from making mistakes.

Is there an area of your life that continually comes up, either in thoughts, dreams, or little niggles at the back of the mind? Do you find yourself discussing it with friends perhaps? Is this an area you feel you need to deal with in any way, or just accept and let it be? If like me, you have something that feels resolved, but quite clearly isn't, perhaps chatting to someone else you trust could enable you to explore your options.

Some of the ways I have come across and used for self-reflective decision-making include:

1. **A letter you write to another person** pouring your heart out, explaining what you need to, perhaps asking for forgiveness, perhaps telling them what you really think of them. It's your letter so go to town, let rip – but this letter isn't sent. You set fire to it (in a safe place, please) or shred it into pieces, then you let go of the contents and draw a line under the experience. This is an immediate closure activity so well worth a try.
2. **A letter you write to another source**, I use the word source because in the book where I read about this exercise, it was to God. As an agnostic, I found I couldn't use God. I asked myself what I did believe in, and the answer was immediate: I believe in Karma. So I write a letter to Karma, like a Dear Diary entry in a way. You outline the issue, the problem, the grievance and pour it all out, no self-editing – this letter is between you and the source you believe in. No one else. You might be asking for help, for ideas or suggestions as to how you resolve the issue. Once you have written the letter in full, and signed off, you then take a fresh page, and you reply to yourself. Start with Dear (your name) and answer the problem in any way you want. Go into as much detail as you can, really go to town with your inner agony aunt or uncle. Sign it off as the source, in my example, Karma.

The second exercise is my favourite one for anytime I am really stuck. I truly believe that we have the answers available to us, that we do know what's best for us as individuals. I just feel that in our hectic lives of work, kids, domestic activities, families, friends, social media, exercise, hobbies – the list goes on – we do not take enough time to think, not deeply and honestly. The reason this exercise works for me and people I have recommended it to, is that it can be done in a short space of time, and as you are giving yourself a private space to work through an issue, it tends to give answers that perhaps you knew were there, but hadn't had the time to fully vocalise or realise.

Try both of the above, and at all times, with any of the exercises we work through, please be kind to yourself. It is of no benefit to yourself to let the gremlin criticise you for not having the answer before. You didn't have the answer, end of. If you have found it now, fantastic, what will you do with it? Ponder for a while, pick up the phone, write a letter, set a goal, whatever feels right for you in your situation should be the outcome. If you feel you have come across a massive issue that requires outside, professional help there is a directory of counsellors to help find someone to deepen your experience.[6]

I started this section talking about forgiving others, however it's also really important to stop any negative gremlin-style rubbish and forgive ourselves at all times. Here's a quick, hopefully easy and useful exercise to check in with yourself where this aspect is concerned:

- Where (in what aspect of your life) do you think you need to forgive yourself?

- Why is that the case?

- Who else is involved in this?

[6] https://www.counselling-directory.org.uk/

- When did this start?

- Can you recall the details of how it started?

- How can you forgive yourself?

- What would you need to do to forgive yourself?

- Can you now let it go?

If the answer to the last question is no, is there someone who can help you further? A friend, trusted colleague, counsellor, coach or another specialist resource? Good job on doing this work, if it was easy everyone would be doing it all the time, and they are certainly not, so you are part of a fairly exclusive club of people owning up to their stuff and choosing to work on it – well done!

CHAPTER SIX

'Life always begins with one step outside of your comfort zone' – Shannon L. Alder

One of the most influential books I have ever been lucky enough to find and read, and pay attention to, is *Feel the Fear and Do it Anyway* by Susan Jeffers. I think I read it back in the 1990s when I was curious about the world of self-help but wasn't particularly engaged with it, that came about a decade later. I really liked that Jeffers thought we could all just do whatever the heck we wanted. I loved that mindset. At that time in my life, I wasn't ready to embrace my fears, but I liked how she spoke to everyone else. I thought she probably helped millions of others, but at the time I was partying too hard, drifting around jobs and generally having a blast and I certainly wasn't ready to actually do any work on myself. You have to be ready.

The fact that you have this book and you are still reading indicates that you are curious about change or improvement – whether it is the right time, only you can answer that. Just try the exercises and see how you find them, see what comes up if you journal, you could chat to someone you trust who will support you. I have changed my friendship groups numerous times because some people influence my thoughts with their negative mindset and I now know the importance of protecting myself and my mental health.

The roles I have taken in my career were chosen because they would be fun and challenge me, they (on the whole) enhanced my well-being and mental health, with the very obvious exception of when I first started teaching teenagers. Perhaps I should give you a little background on how I ended up responsible for hundreds of students and their journey from GCSE to university-entry level. Put simply: by accident. As I have found throughout my life, if I focus on doing what makes me happy in my work life, things just turn up. Don't get me wrong, I have to go looking for them, or do something to make that happen. To quote Steve Jobs again, 'You can't connect the dots looking forward; you can only connect them looking backwards.'

My work life is a scattered mess of a CV which has been a teensy weeny bit tailored to disguise some of my most appalling failures and rubbish decisions. But from all of that, I am where I am, and I wouldn't be anywhere else. So, what was the accident that got me into teaching? Again, let's provide some context. My adoptive mum was a teacher and I recall that holidays, weekends and evenings for her meant books, marking and not a lot else. That put me off, funnily enough. Fast forward to my early forties and a redundancy from a very prestigious but 'not really me as it was dull as heck' office job followed by a stint in counselling paid for by the now ex-employer in order to 'explore my opportunities'.

What was I to do now that I was unemployed and in possession of a lump sum? Enter counsellor. During the counselling session, I realised that because of my upbringing, where I did not attend school full-time until I was eleven years of age, I had a deep feeling of not having the qualifications I deserved. And by deserved, I mean that I knew I was capable of achieving. Due to only entering the mainstream education system at eleven (at the time of my adoption), I had managed to get a few GSEs and CSEs, but by returning to evening classes often I managed to top up my handful. At this time, away from any parental or societal expectations, I did the courses that I loved. I got an A* in drama, don't you know. I took photography – I remember calling someone and telling them I got a B. Their response? Why didn't you get an A? I think it was around this time, I started to only share information with people I knew would see the opportunity to congratulate and support. I also did psychology and sociology, because they were interesting not because I needed them for a job application. I loved learning, and looking back, I could have done more qualifications, but I was saving myself for the big one.

In that counselling session I realised I wanted to prove I could get a degree. My adoptive mum was the only person in either my natural or adoptive families to go to university in the way you are 'supposed' to, from A levels. Ah, A levels, I didn't have any, and as much as I was proud of all those evening class qualifications, I wanted to take on the challenge of a degree. I left the counselling session and walked to the local adult education college and signed up for an access course, the route one takes when one is over twenty-one years of age and has no A levels. The psychology course was full. Damn. I didn't want to wait for a year to get a space, I wanted to start this now, so I signed up for education as you know, teaching is a career and I kind of thought that by now, I would actually have one of those.

Did I plan to be a teacher then? I think it was an option, but I just really wanted to get into university. But I didn't have maths. Not even a CSE. So I started the maths GCSE course alongside the access course and also worked part-time. The year flew by and suddenly we had to apply to real universities. Where I lived in Brighton, there are two. The University of Sussex and Brighton University. I only wanted to go to Sussex, because it has the best reputation, and I felt that with the range of courses they had I would be best placed on the Theatre Studies and English Literature course.

Why? Because of my A* in drama and the fact that my highest qualification at school way back in 1983 was English Literature. I got an A in that. Might as well not only play to my strengths but enjoy the three years which were about to cost me over £20,000. The prospect of studying at this level coupled with the fear of making a huge mistake plus spending all that money was a massive issue for me. I tried to focus on the fact that I really wanted to do this. I had told someone else that this was what I wanted, and I had done that deliberately because for many years I had let my fears hold me back. I had the counsellor to chat to in follow-up sessions, and she said quite plainly, 'if that's what you want to do – what's stopping you?' I realised the answer was loud and clear: it's me, I am stopping me. I had to get out of my own way and get on with it. Facing fears isn't something any of us stop and decide to do too frequently. But we really can benefit from looking at what's holding us back.

At that time in my life, if you had asked me to write down my fears my list would have looked like this:

1. Fear that I am not clever enough.
2. Fear that everyone will be younger and I won't fit in.
3. Fear that I can't return to studying after all these years.
4. Fear that I'll get kicked out for not being good enough.
5. Fear that I won't be able to afford to live on a student loan – I have a mortgage and bills.
6. Fear that it's a mistake and a waste of time.
7. Fear that I will have to work part-time alongside the course.

Can you name your fears around a certain aspect of your life? Don't worry if you can't come up with seven. It's just good to open up (even if only to yourself) about what is frightening to you about an area of your life. It could be fears around joining a gym, starting a new job, getting married, getting divorced, planning a family – anything at all. Perhaps scribble some notes down and lay out your fears for your eyes only.

I knew I was scared, and in counselling I was encouraged to explore my fears. This is what I decided upon in order to counteract them:

1. I am clever, I just don't have the qualifications to prove it.
2. They will be a lot younger but that's OK, I get along with people and that's all they are: people.
3. I won't know unless I try – I can buy books on study skills.
4. I will be good enough, I will work hard and I will do what it takes.
5. I could look for live-in jobs and rent my flat out.
6. I will be studying two subjects I love – I will end up with a degree.
7. I am capable of working hard for three years and doing what it takes.

Would you like to find some ways to redress your own fears? If so, what statements would be useful for to counterbalance the fears you have discovered? Can you write them down now in your pad? Use the above to guide you if you feel stuck. If it helps, chat to someone you trust to help you, sometimes outside perspective is useful.

The reality of my situation is as follows:

1. I was clever enough – I got a much higher degree than I thought I could.
2. I was the oldest, and that was beneficial, when working with my much younger peers I had age, wisdom and experience on my side and I helped and supported anyone who needed it.
3. I did it, I returned to studying and I loved it and was good at it – eventually.
4. I didn't get kicked out – not even close!
5. I worked part-time by taking on many jobs and I paid my mortgage and bills.
6. It wasn't a mistake, they were three of the best years of my life.

7. Yes, I worked part-time alongside, it was very tiring but I did it.

I actually got a 2:1 degree and was over the moon, I remember sitting in an apartment with my sister Freya in Barcelona. I had won two free tickets to the city when EasyJet launched their Gatwick to Barcelona route on the local radio station, the clue was: Which popstar is to be found spinning around? Thank God for years hanging out in Brighton's gay clubs, it was Kylie! I was first through on the phone and won two return tickets. I clearly remember being sat on the floor in this Airbnb we had booked, with really, really slow wi-fi, logging on to the university website to get my final grades for my dissertations, and I truly and utterly believed I had failed and would get a third-class degree or have to redo the whole thing. I had needed to work throughout my degree (which is not advised). I worked six days a week in six different jobs – childcare for two families, cleaning jobs in three households and running chocolate workshops.

Getting the degree was without a shadow of a doubt, the most ridiculously hard thing I have ever done, and at this stage in my life, I had run two businesses and I thought that was tough. Being a mature student meant I was double the age of everyone in all my seminars, workshops and lectures. I remember the first time I sat behind two students in their pyjamas at 2 p.m. in the afternoon in a lecture of world-class renown (it was Sussex, they do not do it any other way) and thought, I do not fit in here. I had not written an essay since 1983, this was 2009. My early attempts at essay writing got me fifty-five per cent as a score. I was not used to this low grades malarkey. I was accustomed to succeeding at pretty much everything I turned my hand to. So, I had to improve, fast. If you failed the first year, it didn't count against your overall grade, but I knew it was a foundation year on which to build in years two and three. If I didn't get the first year under my belt and feel good about it, I was going to have a tough time in the two that followed.

I remember going to my academic advisor and telling him I was thinking of giving up. He asked how long I had felt this way. I replied, about a week. He said come back when that's months and we will talk. No nonsense, I like it. So, I just got on with it, I spent hours in the library, I read everything I could while some of my party-going nineteen-year-old peers drank loads of red bull or coffee the night before a deadline and pulled a ninety per cent essay out of their laptops. How? Yes, I admit I was jealous, but I wasn't able to create work without a lot, literally weeks and weeks, of research and editing. What really helped me get through this was getting a mentor. The university simply paired you with someone. *When you asked for help*. I let my stupid ego and pride get in the way until the third year. My mentor proofread, critiqued and encouraged, but never ever gave me the answers. She was amazing and I wish I had asked for help earlier. Perhaps I would have got a first-class honours degree? But I didn't and I was over the moon with a 2:1. I was so, so proud and I was in Barcelona with my wonderful sister Freya to celebrate. And celebrate we did.

Let's pause there: Who could *you* ask for help, support or a listening ear that you are avoiding asking for 'some reason'? For me it was 'stupid ego and pride'. I was older, experienced, and basically I thought it was a sign of weakness to ask for help. I actually laugh out loud at these words now, I got out of my own way at university (eventually) and I got that mentor, who could be a 'mentor' to you? When are you going to contact them? Could you do it now?

So I have my degree. Now what? Unfortunately, as any recently graduated member of the public will tell you, you do not, as I thought, have a golden ticket in your hand to launch the most amazing career once you collect your certificate. But I had done it and that was, the best feeling I have ever had. This is where Mum, bless her, did the most surprising thing. She called to tell me she was very proud and that, as a treat, I could expect a payment into my bank account. I am used to Mum popping money in my bank account at Christmas and for my birthday, she knows that I never waste special occasion money on frivolous things, I have to have something to show for it. I got quite excited at the thought of a facial or a new top. When I checked my bank, Mum had put £1,000 into my account.

I called to check it wasn't a mistake, perhaps she had pressed too many zeros? She assured me that she'd made no error, and was so proud of me for my years of hard work, leaving a job market to become a student and taking the hardships that went with it for the duration. I was speechless, and anyone who knows me well can vouch for my ability to talk. Mum thought I could pay off a few debts and treat myself to something nice too. I had other ideas. I was exhausted, I honestly have never felt as tired in my life – the focus, hard work and concentration had left me feeling wiped out. I popped to STA Travel on the high street and chatted to a chap about flights.

When I called Mum to tell her I had spent the money, she was delighted I was taking some time out. I have a brother who lives in Bangkok and I was flying there in six weeks' time. Mum was thrilled, no doubt thinking of taking up half my luggage allowance with presents for my nieces. I remember her saying, 'Oh darling, a holiday! How long are you going for?' A year, I replied. There was a silence on the phone, I take it she thought it was a bad connection and she had misheard. So, as I am prone to do, I filled the silence, explaining that I had been very sensible, I had spent £800 on a return ticket into Kuala Lumpur in Malalysia and back out of Bangkok in Thailand, but that the other £200 had gone on travel insurance, the flight could be changed up to three times for no extra cost, but it was currently fixed to come back in a year's time. Her reply? 'But you have no money, how will you live?' Good question. My reply probably freaked her out, but she hid it well. Overdraft and credit cards. She got off the phone quite quickly, which was OK, I had to pack up and get myself ready for an adventure.

Why did I decide to go off for a year? Because I could. Without Mum's money, it would never have happened. It just felt right and it was another time in my life that I look back on with zero regrets and a million memories. So, my question to you is: what could you do just because you find yourself in a position that you can do it? Is there some burning idea that you've ignored for too long? A book? A business? A trip to some far-flung location? Let yourself dream and make notes or journal about this now, and who knows what your 'because I could' might be.

Let's pause for an exercise – please note that some of these questions ask you to dig deep, hopefully you are used to that now, but please be kind to yourself, if a question does not feel comfortable, leave it – return to it another time when you are ready.

- What have you always dreamed of doing?

- What goals or dreams have you put on a back burner that you are actually quite passionate about?

- What do you tell yourself you would do if only [insert reason here]?

- Can you write out your absolute ideal day? Be as detailed as possible. Start with where you wake up, the environment, who is there with you, what you eat, where you go (for example work, the gym, a spa, shops). Explore each part of your day – the more detail you can go into the better.

- If you only had a year to live, what would you do?

- Imagine yourself at ninety years of age, what would you tell your younger self?

- Eulogy exercise: some people don't like this one, but if you are OK to try it, it can be powerful for flushing out ideas. What do you want your loved ones to say about you at your funeral? What would your life have been like? What would you have achieved? What is the legacy that you leave behind?

With all of the above ideas, dreams, fantasy: it is what you have decided to write down, so please try not to be too hasty to disregard any of it as impossible to attain. Why not consider the TGROW model and explore something further, why not actually give it a go here?

When I did the exercise about my ideal day, it included (amongst other things) yoga, meditation, writing and a very long lazy lunch. At the time of doing the exercise none of those things featured in my life. As I write here today – OK, a good few years later – all of them do. Did I just plant a seed that day? Did I actually reach the conclusion that I really wanted these things in my life? Yes, to both. If you want to achieve something quickly then TGROW needs to reflect that in terms of the timing, way forward section. For me, I can sometimes be really slow to adopt things, it's just the way I am, but hey, I get there. You will get there too. Just be realistic and look at your opportunities, don't forget who can help and please, if it's really making you excited to just think about making a dream, idea or fantasy a reality – go for it! Make it happen. For you. Consider it a gift to yourself.

CHAPTER SEVEN

'I never lose. I either win or learn' – Nelson Mandela

As you might have realised as I told you about my time at university, I was really hung up on being the best and, as the oldest, getting it right and not asking for help. I was clearly not in a place where I was happy to make mistakes. In fact I worked hard to be so self-sufficient that I only found out my errors once the essay had been graded – by that point they counted towards my final grade and were unfixable. The only regret I have is not reaching out for help, I thought I was struggling because it was all new to me – yes, it was new and, therefore, I simply did not know the tricks and tips on how to research, how to write, how to assimilate information, how to edit, how to study better and faster, how to skim and scan, how to reference.

That's a long list of things I didn't know how to do and as a proud, capable person, I didn't realise for two years that someone who had been on the same degree as me could help by mentoring, proofreading and supporting. Why did I take this long to ask for help? Because I was not OK with making mistakes. I was so hard on myself, I expected to shine, be the best and I wasn't being very realistic about what I could and couldn't do. We all have areas of our life that we expect to master, we need that validation of ourselves. I love proving to myself I can do something. It gives me a nice warm feeling and the motivation to keep going. But becoming OK with mistakes? That's a tough one for me, and yet it is so liberating when you allow yourself to make them.

The thing I found out was once I allowed myself to get it wrong, it was easier for myself or someone else to spot and then all we had to do was find a solution. So making a mistake can actually be the easiest way to success. Lots of famous people will tell you all about how their missteps enabled them to grow and develop, but if like me you found yourself resistant to making them in the first place, you are not benefitting from the learning available.

One of the most effective ways of dealing with this, is to put yourself in a situation outside of your comfort zone. Your comfort zone is the place where you are good at what you do and you tend to get things right. Move out of that zone, and very soon, a mistake will arrive. When I returned from my year backpacking and working around Asia, I had no idea where to use my degree or how to return to a nine-to-five world having just inhabited a very different one. I needed to get a job but I didn't know what to do. So I made my first error. I went back to office work. I took temporary positions from an agency so that I could move around and experience different cultures, see what was out there and experience all that was on offer. But then I made my second mistake. I took a long-term contract in one place, and soon became a nine-to-fiver with a fixed salary, set of expectations and a job role.

I didn't love the job, and found myself moaning to Freya about how stupid I felt not using my degree and being stuck doing something I was less than passionate about. I was lucky enough to have the support and advice of someone I trusted, my sister was a great sounding board. She simply stated what was really obvious, but I was too caught up in moaning to stop and notice: 'It sounds like you need a change.' The change I made was to start my own business, again. With this business, I had all the mistakes of the first one to learn from, not repeat, and use to help me make this one more successful. And it was. I enjoyed running this company much more, and I applied the lessons from the mistakes to the business model from day one.

Previous business mistake 1
Cash flow running out
How to avoid in this new business
Worked an additional part-time job from day one
The result
Guaranteed income to support growth of business
The opportunity from the mistake
Peace of mind, business had a stronger foundation

Previous business mistake 2
Poor book-keeping
How to avoid in this new business
Thorough monthly checks of bank account, outgoings and income
The result
Able to adapt business goals to address shortfalls and use profits to invest wisely
The opportunity from the mistake
Knew when to order supplies and when to hold off

Previous business mistake 3
Purchasing items I never used
How to avoid in this new business
Implemented a 'don't buy anything until book-keeping is done' policy
The result
Rarely wasted money
The opportunity from the mistake
Purchasing became a monthly consideration not daily so more controlled

Previous business mistake 4
Long hours and no work–life balance
How to avoid in this new business

Allocated time to a) work on the business, b) work in the business and c) do part-time salaried role

The result

Worked about forty hours a week

The opportunity from the mistake

Plenty of time to enjoy my social life and hobbies

Previous business mistake 5

Geographical challenge

How to avoid in this new business

Worked further afield to encourage more customers

The result

Needed a car and extra costs came with this but that was accounted for

The opportunity from the mistake

Knew I needed to cover a larger area to increase potential

Can you look back and see where mistakes turned into opportunities for you? It doesn't have to be on the scale I have described by starting a business. It's just useful to note that mistakes can provide opportunity, so I encourage us all to be happier about making them and not so hung up on getting it right. Because it might not be right after all.

Let's get you working on this – it might just produce some interesting answers, I hope so:

What mistakes have you made?

What happened in each example?

Looking back, can you identify any opportunities, however small, that arose from those experiences?

Again, please take a minute to congratulate yourself on doing that, these might be getting easier, or not, we are all different and we all have a unique approach to digging deep. But you are still here, reading and working away on you – that's great, really well done.

CHAPTER EIGHT

'You can't go back and change the beginning, but you can start where you are and change the ending' – James Sherman

About three years ago I went through one of the most awful work-based experiences of my life. I was signed off with stress for months so I had a lot of time on my hands, too much time. My gremlin had a field day and my ability to block out what was happening at work was very hard, it consumed me and took over my every thought. Fortunately I met an amazing doctor who looked after me and kept me in a safe place – out of the workplace. He advised me to really think about my self-care. I remember that I was in his consulting room, in tears (that was a constant at this time), and I had just bought a bunch of beautifully coloured flowers to cheer myself up. I indicated to the doctor that the blooms were my self-care, and he said gently I might need a little more than that. I heart the NHS. (Thank you, Sam – you were an angel in disguise that day.)

I had attended a day's meditation course at the local Buddhist centre the previous month. On a walk to the park, I had spotted their brochure which advertised a half-day course on 'death and dying'. Not the most cheerful subject, I am sure you'll agree. As I write this book, I have just said goodbye to my twenty-three-year-old cat, Billy. Back then, when I saw the advert I decided to try it out, after all cats tend to live until the sixteen or seventeen year mark so I knew Billy was on borrowed time. Could a Buddhist approach to death help me when the time came?

I loved that course, I actually sat and giggled through most of it. Inappropriate? Not at all. Gen Kelsang Thekchen, a Canadian monk based at the centre, was leading the course and he was hilarious. He made everything so accessible and I left feeling very confident that when the time came I would feel sad to lose my precious cat, but I would cope as I identified with the Buddhist belief that we reincarnate. I was right to trust I would cope, as Billy left this planet, I cuddled him and wished him well on his journey and told him how loved he was here and how loved he would be there. Wherever 'there' is.[7]

I don't think you have to decide to adopt a religion if you like what it says, but I walked in there sceptical and came out thinking that it all made sense to me, and I am now very open to Buddhist beliefs. When Sam, the doctor, said self-care, and after the flowers had wilted and been thrown away, I realised I had a Buddhist centre up the road and that an easy to afford opportunity to work on myself was available. I went on a five-day partially silent meditation course there. Until this point, I had used Headspace, which is a ten-minute guided meditation app, twice.[8] So, I went from ten minutes a day, which I admit I struggled with, to attending five days of teachings and mediation that ran from 9 a.m. to 9 p.m. I was exhausted. I never realised that meditating took it out of you so much. We were invited to focus our breath. For hours and hours. We had a break after lunch for a couple of hours and I went home and got into bed and slept. For me, it was the only way to get through until 9 p.m. without falling asleep on my chair. The course was the best thing I could have done. Was I then an expert meditator? No. Not at all. My gremlin is strong. I have fed it well over the years and given it lots of reasons to chat

---

[7] The course I took was at the Bodhisattva Kadampa Meditation Centre – they do day-, weekend-, week- and month-long, drop-in and residential courses. I even saw some virtual ones on their website – check them out at meditateinbrighton.com

[8] Headspace is a fantastic app and you get a free ten-day trial – try it out at headspace.com

away about all sorts of deeply personal, wounding and hurtful rubbish.

Over lockdown one and the crazy year that ensued, my goals were to a) write this book and b) meditate for fifteen minutes a day every day. I have stuck at it for over a year! I am amazed, but I have loved it. I use Insight Timer[9] but you do not have to use an app, you can simply find a comfortable position where you won't be disturbed.

Turn off all radios, phones, tablets and TVs. Set a timer (if using phone, activate the do not disturb feature) and just focus on your breath as you breathe in and out. That's it, that's meditation. Try counting how many breaths you get to before your thoughts invade. Mine is around three. Yes, even now after lots more sessions at the centre and apps and trying really, really hard to get it right. Bloody thoughts creep in every time. And as Headspace and monks and Insight Timer people will tell you – it's OK. Let the thoughts go, just observe them arriving, and don't engage with any of it. Then go back to the breath. I find counting my breaths backwards from one hundred focuses me. Not all the time, as I said that gremlin and my thoughts are strong.

I recently read *The Doctor Who Sat for a Year* by Brendan Kelly, a book which manages to be very funny alongside detailing one man's journey as he tried to meditate for a year. It inspired me to do regular meditations, and I can honestly say that it helps. I feel calmer, more centred and despite the thoughts rushing in, I do have some lovely peaceful moments. I would highly recommend that you try meditation out.

Peaceful moments have become somewhat of a calming balm in my life, and I have taken to spending a lot more time by myself than ever before. At first I felt guilty, that 'to do' list always niggles at the back of my mind. I try to ignore it and tell myself it will all get done (it does actually) but the gremlin is busy nagging

---

[9] Another brilliant app someone on the five-day retreat told me about – insighttimer.com

me. Meditation helps me to ignore that. The other things that I have tried and tested and can offer to you as ‘worth trying out’ are the following.

A gratitude journal. Just before I go to sleep at night I scribble down ten things that I am grateful for during that day. Recently I have added three things I have achieved that day. Appreciating the little things has a snowball effect, it leads to greater contentment overall. Having enough to eat, some pretty nice things to wear and a roof over my head can be taken for granted. When I backpacked through South East Asia, I continually saw people living in cardboard boxes at the side of the road, so being grateful for the ‘birth lottery’ whereby I was given this Western life as opposed to another, is worth having a moment of gratitude for, in my opinion.

Learn something. Currently I am struggling to learn Spanish. In 1990 whilst based in Menorca, I invested in a linguaphone course and when I got to my place on the island used it for about a week. Knowing one day I would want to ‘get my money’s worth’, I never threw it out and recently started doing thirty minutes a day. Have I embraced this learning wholeheartedly? Not a chance. I actually have to bribe myself with rewards to sit down and get on with it. The crazy thing is, once I start I absolutely love it. I have used the TGROW exercise to understand why the heck I am procrastinating over something I set myself as a goal, and the conclusion is, I would rather be reading a book. So I have had to bribe myself. If I do five consecutive days, I earn a reward. It’s working. Don’t be afraid to reward yourself if that is what motivates you to get something done. On the other hand, you might want to choose a goal that is more aligned to your motivations, I am clearly not that interested in learning Spanish, I am more invested in not wasting the money the linguaphone course took from my bank account. Thirty years ago. If we meet, don’t be surprised if I am not fluent in Spanish.

Admit what you can't change. Some things just are beyond our control. We might work hard on something and for whatever reason, it still does not work out. I think that we are all entitled to try and fail. A lot. It's from these failures that some really good self-development can occur. I tried to work full-time in the education system. I did it for a handful of months. Then I realised that even with my superb organisational skills, ability to put the hours in and desire to be the best teacher I could be, this was bigger than me. It took bursting into tears in front of a student (fortunately, it was just the one student) to make me stop and take a good hard look at what the system and its ridiculous expectations were doing to my sanity and work–life balance. I now work part-time.

Be kind, be compassionate and be thoughtful. Kindness need not be fancy gifts, it can be the small things that show you have kind thoughts towards another. Remembering someone has a job interview and sending them luck is thoughtful. Baking enough cakes or biscuits for you plus others is a good way to show you care. Compassion towards others is a great habit to cultivate, if someone is behaving in a way that I find objectionable, I try to stop and remember that I have no idea of their upbringing or circumstances. Remaining a good person and caring towards another who is in a bad place will, I guarantee, make you feel great.

Get off your phone. I was brought up on pen and paper, and I, therefore, do not have the attachment to my phone that perhaps other generations do. Regardless of your reliance on your device, having a holiday from it is highly recommended. As someone who used social media to raise awareness of her businesses, I have seen the positives and unfortunately the negatives of being linked to all and sundry via the wonders of the web. Currently I use social media to help share the fact I have written this book as I wish as many people to know about it as possible. But in the past I have come off social media completely – this was a choice I made when viewing various platforms took over hours of my life. It then left me feeling that I was living a pretty poor imitation of life, compared to all these glossy fabulous humans that popped up in my feed. I detoxed for years, then found a way to return to suit me. You do not have to be all or nothing, you can do what works for you, but it's very healthy to have some time out to use your brain for other activities.

Read books. Matt Haig has a wonderful selection of books that (in my opinion) should grace all bookshelves. His *Notes on a Nervous Planet* addresses the social media addiction beautifully and would benefit anyone. I would also recommend *Live Happy* by Dr Ilona Boniwell and Bridget Grenville-Cleave. In which the authors share simple ways to add joy to our lives. If you have not come across the Dalai Lama's cat series by David Michie, I am jealous that you have this experience to come. They are the most beautiful stories weaving the beauty of Buddhist beliefs into a cute tale about a kitten saved by the Dalai Lama. I recently bought the complete set for one of my friends who helped me out by reading a draft version of this book. They make fab presents. Paulo Coelho is another treat awaiting you if you have not yet discovered his books. I started with *The Alchemist* and I am working my way through his catalogue. Finally, have you come across *The Little Book of Hygge* and *The Little Book of Lykke*? Also 'must reads', there are three books in total, the third is *The Art of Making Memories*. I highly recommend them, not only for the fantastic content, but for the very amusing way Meik Wiking tells his stories, I giggle throughout and learn at the same time. The author is the founder of the Happiness Institute in Copenhagen. Yes, there is an institute for happiness, I want to visit immediately!

So, over to you, can you think of just five things to try to help you with your own self-care needs?

Just having these firm ideas that help you when you need a bit of TLC (tender loving care) and giving yourself a self-care half-hour can make the difference between looking after yourself and putting it off in favour of that pesky 'to do' list. Ignore the chores, and focus on you. You won't regret it.

If you wish to try these books, here are some links for you.

Brendan Kelly ,*The Doctor Who Sat for a Year* by https://amzn.to/3A9UcJL
Matt Haig, *Notes on a Nervous Planet* https://amzn.to/2T1qV48
Dr Ilona Boniwell and Bridget Grenville-Cleave, *Live Happy: 100 simple ways to fill your life with joy* https://amzn.to/3jUWUOu
David Michie, The Dalai Lama cat series https://amzn.to/3dZZpva
Paulo Coelho, *The Alchemist* https://amzn.to/3hqQ3dN
Meik Wiking, *The Little Book of Hygge* https://amzn.to/2UyQeLp
Meik Wiking, *The Little Book of Lykke* https://amzn.to/36E06Gx
Meik Wiking, *The Art of Making Memories* https://amzn.to/3hP4RlH

CHAPTER NINE

A mistake repeated more than once is a decision – Paulo Coelho

I came across a really interesting premise recently, and that is self-sabotage. I was on the mailing list of a coach called Vivienne Joy and she invited me to join her seven-day self-sabotage coaching course. I could have joined the Facebook group and completed each day at the same time as everyone else, but I was busy so I just worked my way through it when I had the time. As a concept, I was very impressed and I ended up with nine new goals I wanted to work on. This would normally really overwhelm me but we were just coming into the coronavirus lockdown in the UK and I thought, wow, great timing, Vivienne. I do not have any excuses, I have lots of time on my hands and the only thing that can stop me is me.

I think the wording grabbed me the most – self-sabotage. Can you honestly put your hand on your heart and say you have never sabotaged yourself? I couldn't, I do it too much and it annoys me that I do. But life is all about choices. What you choose to do with your life will ultimately lead to the outcome of it. You can decide to do exactly what you are doing now, and perhaps that's what you want. But if you are reading this book for the reason it was written, to shake things up a bit, gain an understanding of how to move forward, actively work on yourself rather than let life happen to you, then you might have some other choices to make.

To quote Henry Ford, 'Whether you think you can or you think you can't, you're right.' So, what do you think? What do you want to do? Nothing? Fine, as long as you are aware that doing nothing is a choice, as long as you are happy with it, then that is great. Carry on doing nothing. In the course that Vivienne ran, she talked about all the different areas of your life that you might see yourself sabotaging. Inspired by her amazing work, I created a selection of my self-sabotage areas from my own Wheel of life:

- Fitness & health
- Money
- Friends and family
- Personal growth
- Career
- Significant other
- Physical environment
- Spirituality

Asking myself how I self-sabotaged was a really powerful question for me, it unearthed a lot of guilt that I have been self-sabotaging for many, many years. I had to work on being kind to myself and almost shrug it off, it's in the past, my time machine is non-existent so I cannot go back and change a blinking thing. I simply have to accept that this is where I am. I approached each category and was very thorough, writing out what I had done, then went on to explore why I had, looked at the benefits of doing so and then setting goals to stop. I am of course simplifying the process – we can look at your self-sabotage efforts here, though I do recommend Vivienne's course for the full guidance she offers.[10]

What are the ways that you self-sabotage in each category? Write them all out in detail.

- Fitness & health

[10] I recommend that you check out her website and see what resources she has available – mindsetforbusiness.co.uk

- Money

- Friends & family

- Personal growth

- Career

- Significant other

- Physical environment

- Spirituality

As an example, I am happy to give you a very basic outline of what my self-sabotages were in each area, and the goals I set to fix each:

- **Fitness & health** – I don't always have a healthy diet, do not do enough exercise and drink too much alcohol. **Goal:** two yoga classes per week plus a daily walk or cycle, go vegetarian and give up booze for three months.
- **Money** – I overspend constantly. **Goal:** set up a monthly budget with categories, write each transaction down and know where my money is going.

- **Friends & family** – I keep people who are not benefiting my life at arm's length. **Goal:** join new Meetup groups, and contact old friends via phone and on social media.
- **Personal growth** – I love to travel and visit new places, and I love to read too. **Goal:** set budget for travel and read daily instead of massive Netflix sessions.
- **Career** – I am currently temping. **Goal:** job hunting on a weekly basis to see what's out there.
- **Significant other** – I am currently single. **Goal:** joining more Meetup groups will introduce new people into my life.
- **Physical environment** – I put off doing housework until it's desperately filthy. **Goal:** do a couple of hours a week.
- **Spirituality** – I know the importance of meditation, but I sometimes forget to do it. **Goal:** set an alarm and make sure it happens daily.

At the time of writing, I have been working on these goals for about ten weeks, and I have been really dedicated to their outcome.

Not all the goals I set felt equally important – for example doing housework, I only had to think about that once a week. But some others needed daily progress – like exercise. I find using the Wheel of Life categories useful, but you can play around with yours to suit you best. Overall, doing this really spurred me on, I think that's because I was ashamed that I had self-sabotaged. Let me share something I am really proud of from doing this, the budget I mentioned for money? It's been eye opening to set one and work so hard at sticking to it. I decided to allocate a set monthly amount, then divide into about twelve sub-sections: they included food, travel, clothes, toiletries, cards and stamps, I even included one for flowers. I love flowers and realistically I spend about a fiver a week on them, so my monthly allowance is £20.

If I pick up a bunch of daffodils for a pound, I deduct that pound from the flowers budget, meaning I don't overspend. In the first month, I went way over on food. This was because we were in lockdown due to Covid-19, and I was using the shops at the top of the road rather than the cheapest ones, so of course I spent more. I simply adjusted where I shopped, as I really didn't want to keep wasting money on more expensive items due to the convenience of the local stores. If money-wasting is a bugbear of yours, this might work for you too. Martin Lewis of Money Saving Expert fame, wrote a fantastic book that I read years ago, all about managing money better: *The Three Most Important Lessons You've Never Been Taught.*

I followed his advice and got out of credit card, overdraft and personal loan debt in only a few years. In fact, three years ago I could not pay my mortgage payment in January. We all overspend at Christmas, but it wasn't that, I was rubbish at managing my money, end of. I lived beyond my means, hence the credit cards, overdraft and loans. I was from the 'let's have it all, I work hard' school of thought. Yes, I do work hard, but if I spend £1,000 a month more than I earn, it's quite easy to see where you quickly get into trouble with money. A friend lent me the Martin Lewis book and the advice and exercises were easy enough to follow, for example: Where does your money go? I scoffed at this, well that was easy. Bills, living, food. He advises that you look at three months of bank statements and actually take a look at where your money goes. I wasn't worried, I knew. Bills, living, food.

I remember sitting with a coffee, coloured pens at the ready with the statements printed out in front of me. Direct debits I would circle green. Any shop name I knew, orange. And ATM withdrawals, red. My statements were a sea of red. I added up all the red cash withdrawals – over £1,500 a month. I had no idea I was taking so much money out. And where the heck was it going? That's the thing, it's very hard to track cash. I was horrified, in one easy to do (though painful at the time) exercise, I had uncovered that I was a very spendy lady and I didn't know what I was spending on. I made a decision to know what my outgoings were. And now I needed to look hard at my direct debits, could they be reduced?

Was I paying too much for my mobile phone? The answer was yes. Was I paying for any services I didn't use? Again, yes. I shaved off some serious money just by being aware of what was going out of my account. Then I looked at my income. It was easy to see that the amount coming in did not support the amount going out. So I had to rectify it. I bought a little notepad and only used cash from that day forward, I literally wrote every single transaction down each time I used my cash budget. If I need to use a debit card, for online purchases for example, then I had to write that down too. I basically had control of my money and as I said, it took me just a few years to completely turn my finances around. At the time of writing I only work part-time and I still have savings in an account, it's not much, a few grand, but I have never ever had savings before. It's a bit embarrassing to admit that. But that's self-sabotage for you. It's worth working on it, you never know where you could be in just a few months' or years' time.

Let's get you working on you now, can you write down what areas you feel you need to tackle having read this chapter?

Any goals to set?

Any actions to take, even if teeny-tiny ones?

What might your next steps be?

Scribble it all out, it'll help you feel in control, I promise. And it might save you a few grand too! Why not start imagining what you would do with all that lovely saved cash? A holiday? New clothes? A car? Pay off an expensive credit card? Start dreaming, we tend to focus on actions that have solid rewards attached, well I do, it might work for you too.

Book link: Martin Lewis, *The Three Most Important Lessons You've Never Been Taught* https://amzn.to/2UgAL2G

CHAPTER TEN

Give the gift of absence to those who do not appreciate your presence

What's that famous line in a Philip Larkin poem? Oh yes, I remember – it's about parents, 'they fuck you up'. I could spend a lot of time in this area detailing past stories to support that statement, but I feel that wouldn't be fair, I am the one sitting writing a book and those that hurt me don't have the opportunity to reply in real time and besides, I am not interested in hanging people out for public scrutiny and judgement. The facts are simple however, I moved around from birth to eleven years of age living in temporary places, squats and festival sites, I very rarely attended school as you need to live somewhere longer than five minutes to register. I was taught how to read and write, and I was an absolute bookworm – to this day I love nothing better than a good book.

At eleven years of age my birth mother moved thousands of miles away to an ashram in India taking two of my younger siblings with her and left myself and one sibling in the UK with our 'dad'. Who promptly left us behind so he could go too. She signed the paperwork in India for my guardianship (akin to adoption) and posted it over. My adoptive parents were not really in a financial position to take in two more mouths to feed, but as decent, kind human beings they did so and I am, of course, very grateful to them. I cannot imagine what might have happened without them making a home for myself and my sister at that stage of our lives. I did however, leave this home at sixteen years of age and met my birth mother in the north of England where we lived like two mates, going out clubbing and getting drunk until she got bored of that town, and off she went again. We no longer have contact. That's another story entirely. So yes, I maintain - 'they fuck you up'. If you let them, of course.

I spoke to a counsellor recently about all aspects of my childhood and she recommended that I have at least a year's therapy in order to deal with the neglect and trauma caused during those years. My response was to have a bloody good cry, then research what was out there to help. I did not feel like attending counselling for so long, and I am aware I was going against the good advice of a trained professional.

My stance on advice is that it is given, but you do not have to take it. How much guidance have you been given over the years that you followed and it still didn't fix things? I have been overly reliant by thinking that the person advising me had *the* answer. What if it was only one of many answers? My research took me to an American psychologist Dr Jonice Webb. I listened to her book, *Running on Empty No More*, in two days. Her website gives a checklist of twenty-one areas of emotional neglect you might identify with, and in her professional opinion if you identify with six or more, you are likely to have been on the receiving end of Childhood Emotional Neglect (CEN). I identified with eight. What I learned was that you don't need a particularly dramatic childhood (such as my own) to have suffered from CEN. In fact, as I listened to the book, I thought that we are all probably likely to have been affected in some way.[11]

The part I found most fascinating was where Webb talked through the different parenting styles and how they manifest in the day to day. She gave examples, and I was pleased at the end of the book to realise it could have been worse! The neglect was

---

[11] If you want to check out Dr Jonice Webb's website to see if CEN might apply to you it is drjonicewebb.com. There are some free resources on there too. The book can be found here: https://amzn.to/3huXIru

something I never realised was there, neglect is the absence of something rather than a tangible thing, which is why it's really hard to identify at the time. This was definitely a book and self-improvement model I needed to come across after my childhood, perhaps a few years earlier would have been useful, but as it was something 'missing' I didn't know it was meant to be there.

The exercises to then heal yourself, and it is healing that needs to take place, are really simple and easy to follow. I started immediately and quite quickly felt calmer and more accepting of what had gone before. The book also spends a lot of time looking at self-care and self-talk. I was pleased that this is an area I have practice in, but it was a good reminder to stop and listen out for the negative self-talk, and stop it. As I have mentioned a lot previously, that inner self-saboteur, the gremlin, is very chatty in my head, and perhaps in yours too? I am all too aware that it does indeed take time, effort and energy to override it. Catching the thought as it arises, and actually replacing it with an opposing, more healthy one is the way to reprogramme the subconscious, it is in this activity that you will feel better. It might feel like hard work, but it can take mere minutes.

My journaling became far more prolific after listening to the book, I really needed to express myself and work through thoughts, past memories and, well, stuff. I made sure to give myself time to do this and do it well. Netflix stayed off for longer until I was happy with the scramble of my old stuff into new healthier more positive ways of thinking about what had gone before. One of the reasons I resisted the advice to stay in counselling for a year was that I try to stay in the now. Oh it's hard; that advice about mindful behaviour sounds oh so simple, and yet, it's positively impossible at times.

Stay in the now, focus on what is around you and what you can see, hear and feel right now. I get the premise, so why is my head bouncing all over the place; from what to eat for dinner, to that conversation that went badly three days ago and where did I leave my phone? To go into counselling and look over the past again and again and again, did not feel like the right thing to do. I might be setting myself up for a longer 'recovery' as I attempt to work on this myself, but know thyself.

I love a good self-improvement book and I have a toolkit bulging with things to try to sort my own head out. Which is the reason I decided to write this book after all. All the items I take out of my toolkit on a daily, weekly and monthly basis, I have simply learned over the years, and if sharing it all with you means that you get to work on the stuff that is important and needs to be worked on, right here, right now, then fantastic, that's two of us on the planet working on being the best versions of ourselves. And that's a pretty amazing place to start.

Has this chapter made you think of anything you might do to help your self-care or healing from any past hurt? What is it? Scribble it all down.

Do you need to make a phone call, research on a website, talk to a friend or family member?

As ever – look after you first, make sure you are doing what you need, then worry about looking after others. Self-care comes first, then try to look after everyone else, you will be more effective if you have worked on your own stuff first. Trust me, I speak from experience.

CHAPTER ELEVEN

Whatever you are not changing, you are choosing – Laurie Buchanan

The subject of my drinking had been causing me concern for as many years as I care to remember. I recall that when I turned forty, the doctors offered a health check so I made an appointment and went along. It was a fairly basic assessment – some tests for cholesterol, weight and height, discussion around diet, blood pressure and then I was asked about my drinking. I was honest and the nurse conducting the health check paused to state the recommended units for a woman per week. Which was about the amount I was drinking per night. At this stage in my life, I visited the off licence at the top of the road every evening on the way back from work where I would collect a four pack of Caffrey's ale for my then boyfriend, and a bottle of Lindeman's Bin 65 Chardonnay for myself. Whilst dinner was being prepared, I would have a glass, then one with our meal, then another watching some TV afterwards. The bottle would be empty by 9 p.m.

I repeated this day in day out, week in week out, not thinking anything of it. I didn't get hangovers, and I went to work and produced the results expected. But the nurse told me categorically that I was drinking way over the recommended limits. She suggested a liver test to see how that was faring. I remember being really nervous about the results. I had been completely honest about the amount I drank during the week, and also shared with her what I consumed whilst partying hard all weekend. The test results showed that I (no surprises) needed to cut down as my liver was not a happy organ.

Around this time, I went to see a homeopath as I was getting frequent bouts of tonsillitis, and I had had very successful results with homeopathy previously. I have suffered with this illness since childhood and unfortunately never had my tonsils taken out. Knowing a course of antibiotics would treat them, but preferring to use alternative remedies where I could, I chatted to the homeopath about my overall health and included the liver test result. She barred me from drinking more than two bottles of wine a week. I took the advice and I decided to drink at the weekend only. The two bottles were often consumed in succession. I grew bored of this as it felt really limiting and I missed the wine, a lot, so I returned to my old habits. The tests on my liver were repeated over the next decade – after the results showed my liver was unhappy I would ease up and cut down a lot and then gradually pick up where I left off. I am not proud of the amount I could consume, but a night out could mean I was drinking around five times the recommended amount of units per week. And I carried on doing this for the next thirteen years. I mentioned before that I am clearly a slow learner in some areas of my life.

When I started university I did some live in work as an au pair and in one job I had a stand-alone annexe to myself which was fabulous, but what I noticed was that as I wasn't sharing with anyone I could happily buy wine in any quantity and consume it in any quantity too. It had been a few years since my liver test but I knew deep down that this was not clever of me, so I asked for some counselling to try and work out the reasons behind my drinking. I went along and after twelve weeks I could only come up with the fact that I had just got into the habit of drinking. It was what all my friends did and it featured so heavily in all areas of my social life, I simply could not see how I would give up and feel like a 'normal' person. And so I didn't bother giving up, I don't think I particularly cut down either. I just carried on until the next liver test gave me a kick up the you-know-what, and I would dutifully reduce my intake until it gradually crept up again.

I had never gone longer than a day or two without a drink since I started drinking when I was about eighteen years of age. Deep down I knew I had a problem, and I didn't know how to stop. I was aware of AA (Alcoholics Anonymous) but I didn't drink until the evening, always after work, I certainly didn't hide my drinking and I never poured vodka onto my cornflakes. So that meant I wasn't an alcoholic, right? But I was 'something'. A binge drinker, probably. I didn't like the control alcohol had over me. I spent a lot of money getting very messy, I often couldn't remember getting home, I spent far too many nights talking absolute rubbish with randoms, I even woke up with a few.

So, I decided to bribe myself. If I could take a whole week off the booze, I was to declare myself definitely not an alcoholic and I would have a £60 fancy handbag from Zara to show for it as a reward. The bag was bought and left in its carrier bag under my dressing table to act as an incentive, I promised my sister Ruth that if I broke the pledge to not drink for seven days, she would have the bag plus receipt and she could go get a refund or keep it. I did the week. It was tough, very tough, I thought of nothing but booze and hated denying myself my lovely Chardonnay, but I did it. I was now (in my mind) not an alcoholic, after all an alcoholic couldn't stop for a week, could they? And so I carried on drinking, and the amounts increased and my behaviour stayed the same.

Until 2019. I was sitting in a car heading on a rural holiday with friends in England. I was telling my mate who was driving us up, that I was fed up with my inability to control my drinking. I had tried setting numbers of units and pacing myself with diluted spritzer-style drinks, pints of water in between the drinks, nights off and the odd month off but I always ended up exactly where I was. Drinking too much and feeling awful – hungover, lethargic, skint, ashamed that I couldn't control myself and just basically, really unhappy with my inability to control or moderate the booze. My friend was experiencing the same sort of thing – she had two kids and noticed that she was always grumpy towards them when hungover and then she felt bad afterwards, so we drew up a pact. We would give up for three months. It seemed huge and I wasn't sure I could do it. Another friend wanted to join us, and so three of us went into the month of September 2019 with the promise to not drink for three months.

The friend who first agreed to join me mentioned a company called One Year No Beer (OYNB) who were 'all over her Facebook feed'. I had left Facebook and any social media so I decided to Google them – they had a website with oodles of resources such as blogs, podcasts and a very active society to join and support one another. I opted for the ninety day booze-free membership, I noticed there were twenty-eight and three hundred and sixty-five days memberships too. How could *anyone* really do a year, I wondered? That's epic and at that point, way beyond my comprehension as to how it was even possible. Given that I had already completed a month off, the twenty-eight days wasn't what I wanted. For the ninety days of the membership I could have joined the Facebook page and shared my experience, but I guess I had my support network in the two pals who were doing the challenge with me.

Month one had me thinking about booze and craving large amounts of it. But if I was tempted I reached out to my pals, and I didn't drink. I had daily emails from OYNB encouraging and educating me as to the way to stay sober. I stayed sober for month two, by this time, I was having feelings that I hadn't truly felt for decades. I would describe them as calm, focus, natural energy and even happiness.

I checked in with my mates, was I the only one feeling different? No, they assured me they felt these things too – we were all just happier. I started to count the other ways I had noticed I was not missing alcohol: no hangovers was the number one, missing days of life to lethargy was up there in the top three, extra money in my account was noticeable, I had lost weight too, my sleep was great and my skin, hair and nails looked healthier. I did month three easily, feeling buoyed up by all this amazing evidence that it was a great thing to do. In December I went back to the booze. At first I was able to drink smaller glasses of wine, pints of sparkling water and single spirits and I was much better for it. Hangovers were far more manageable, I remembered the evenings and had a great time. But I slid, oh, did I slide. Within weeks alcohol had taken control and I was back to consuming my old amounts and regretting it dreadfully. I saw December out with plenty of boozy party-filled nights and wasted days with hangovers so I decided to do dry January. But then back to the booze in February and March. Back straight to my old, by now unavoidable to ignore, unchangeable ways of drinking. I did not control booze, it controlled me.

The last night I drank was Saturday 21st March 2020. I was so drunk that I do not remember much after the taxi to get to the nightclub. The next day I was the most ill I have ever been after consuming alcohol. I had really poisoned myself this time. Despite that, I didn't decide to give up forever. I did however decide to take another three months off and think about what to do next. I felt like a complete failure. In order to evaluate what was going on I decided to list what I had tried and failed at: abstaining pending liver function tests, counselling, diluting drinks, having a unit count per week, any kind of moderation. Conversely, what had worked was financial self-bribery and rewards, peer support and the One Year No Beer membership. I knew I could do three months so I felt that this wasn't even a hard goal to set. The UK was entering lockdown due to Covid-19 and everyone I knew had decided to drink their way through it. I felt that if I did so, I had real potential to undo any good work I had managed thus far. I decided to calculate the average weekly amount of money I had spent on booze during the last couple of weeks and then put a three month's worth into a savings account.

I promised myself that if I drank, the money would go to charity. If I managed the three months, I would use the money to fly out of the UK after lockdown. A weekend away, part-payment on a holiday – it didn't matter. It was something to aim for.

Part of my lockdown was to read like a crazy woman, I downloaded and read three books at a time. Some were to do with alcohol and how to give up or moderate it. Allen Carr's *The Easy Way to Control Alcohol* felt a tad drawn out, I finished it but didn't know if I was returning to booze or not yet. I started a couple of books that annoyed me, I won't mention them here as I am sure they are loved by others. In the end it wasn't strictly a book that helped me decide, it was two other things: a conversation with a colleague and the podcasts on the OYNB website. A woman at work mentioned she tried dry January three years ago and never went back to booze. I was gobsmacked. How on earth did she manage that? She educated herself was her reply. She suggested some titles and I started to listen to the OYNB podcasts every night as I cooked dinner. Suddenly I just knew, me and booze had reached the end of our time together. It didn't bring anything to the party anymore.

I deserved these feelings of happiness, clarity and focus, calm and energy. As soon as I started to drink, they went away again. I chose that, it was that simple for me. A feeling of huge relief swept my entire body, like a weight had been lifted and I felt euphoric, no more month off, few months on, bit of reward here, a hangover there, no more not knowing if I had a real problem with my liver, no more anxiety – as I said, just pure relief and happiness. I won't drink again, it's a gift to myself and my future life and I am so excited about proving to myself that I can do it. Because I can. It's taken since my fortieth-year health check until now to change this behaviour of mine, that's over thirteen years, but I was simply not ready for it until now. I am just so glad that I finally am. There will be the inevitable conversations with people who cannot comprehend life without booze, I was one of them so I know what it feels like, non-drinkers are just weird right?

Some of those I have told have congratulated me, some have stayed quiet and one or two have said, 'I need to sort my drinking out, too.' Wherever you are on your journey, you will get there when you are ready, as I did. If it's an area that bothers you, then I can honestly say that you will find your own answers. Why we drink is so complex and needs to be unpicked and unravelled. Your only action and exercise on this is to be honest with yourself and do what you know you need to do. There is a lot of stuff out there and education is key. If I had to choose a book to start you off, it would be Annie Grace's: *The Naked Mind*. She is a genius is all I am saying. I wish you well on your journey.[12]

Update: as of July 2021 I am still sober, still incredibly happy and I have saved £3,800 according to my app. Just saying.

---

[12] Some resources I found helpful: oneyearnobeer.com, Allen Carr's *The Easy Way to Control Alcohol*, https://amzn.to/3yDUVCf Kevin Laye's *Positive Drinking*, https://amzn.to/3k0joh1

Annie Grace's *The Naked Mind* https://amzn.to/3ANErcq and Russell Brand's *Recovery: Freedom from our Addictions https://amzn.to/3ANHgu4*

CHAPTER TWELVE

'Everything you want is just outside your comfort zone' – Robert G. Allen

The Covid-19 lockdown has been one of the most productive times of my life. I feel like I've used it to reach a range of conclusions in quite a lot of areas. It's given me a lot of hope for being able to do this at other times in my life, obviously I won't have an enforced reason to stay home and work on my stuff, I will simply need to choose to do so. We all know that what we choose to do is up to us. Three hours on Netflix or read a book? Go and workout or consume a tub of ice cream? End up down a social media rabbit hole or write a few pages of a novel? It's all ours for the choosing. I may not work full-time again for a while, I am managing my finances to make this happen, and I love the time for myself – it's a gift to me. I am very grateful to only work part-time and be able to pay my bills. If I go back to work full-time, I am aware that I might never tackle another range of goals like the ones I have dealt with over lockdown, and what a shame that would be. My suggestion (to myself) is don't try to do too much. That way I can really enjoy a new challenge without getting frustrated at my lack of progress. For me, it is better to do something well and enjoy it than force myself to plough through loads of tasks and end up resenting them.

If, like me, you choose to work on yourself going forward, then you are going to have to leave your comfort zone. Often. When you start to recognise why you are unhappy or what needs to change, you take a step towards that new goal and it feels odd and at times, unpleasant. This is where lots of people let the discomfort take over and decide that they are OK where they are. They stop and consequently fail to achieve what they had set out to do. Stepping outside of what is comfortable is needed in order to grow, there are many charts depicting comfort zones and growth on the internet.

They depict a four-step pathway to success:

1. Comfort zone
2. Fear zone
3. Learning zone
4. Growth zone

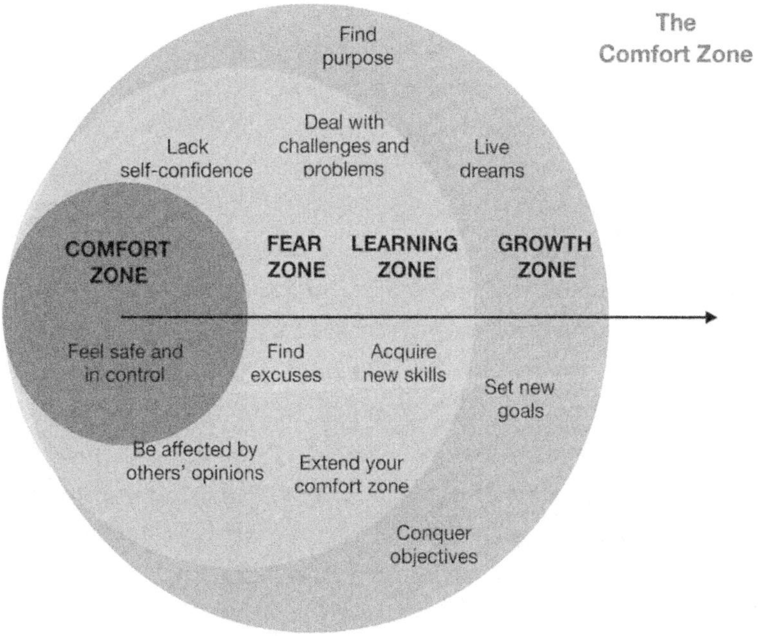

This model suggests that you move from your comfort zone (where you are content with what you know and are safe and happy) onto the second, the fear zone, where you find excuses for not moving forward anymore and where you lack the confidence you had when in the comfort zone. You then move to the third zone, which is the space of learning, and finally you enter your growth zone.

Let's look at an example of how this could work in real life. The goal is giving up alcohol. In the comfort zone the individual is happy to drink thirty to forty units of booze per week, sometimes more. They know the UK recommended amount is way below that (fourteen units for both men and women per week).[13]

They've been told how bad booze is for them but they tried cutting down and it was hard to stick to so they've carried on. Deep down they know it's bad for their health and their finances and so they've decided to give up altogether – they then go into the fear zone. They are scared life won't be interesting without booze because everyone they know, with very few exceptions, drinks so how will they enjoy life sober? The sooner the client enters the learning zone the better, after all knowledge is power. By learning about how others have given up successfully, managed social situations without booze and reaped the benefits of hangover-free days and extra cash to spend on other things, their resolve to give up is strengthened. It can take a lot of research and learning but the more they spend time reading and listening to resources the stronger their determination can become.

They then put the advice into practice – they are now in the growth zone. If they fail at their goal they go back to the fear zone, doubting they can do it, looking at how lacking their ability is and worrying about how realistic it is to take on this goal. So they go back to learning, listen to more podcasts, read more books, gather more knowledge about those who have gone before and succeeded. This motivates and inspires and now they are in the growth zone again, trying once more to achieve the goal.

---

[13] nhs.uk/live-well/alcohol-support/calculating-alcohol-units

However, rather than following this zone 'one to four' approach, I feel the key to getting out of the fear zone is to get the learning lined up immediately. I would say that in order to get the best results, the comfort and learning zones could take first and second place and we remove the fear zone at this stage. It's the fear about failing that can stop us in our tracks.

You remain aware that the fear zone is in existence but you simply ignore it until you've done your research. If the goal of giving up alcohol is too challenging and, therefore, preventing you achieving it, change it to a more realistic one for you. Perhaps cutting down on your screen time? Reducing the number of coffees you drink per day? Doing the Couch to 5k? By working on another goal that feels less scary, you build confidence in your ability, and increase your chances of success at the bigger, more intimidating objective. Whatever goal is selected, firstly you will identify where you are comfortable with it.

State your goal (for the purpose of this exercise).

How can you identify that you are in your comfort zone where this goal is concerned?

Name all the benefits of reaching this goal.

Where could you learn more about achieving this goal?

When will you do the learning required?

How will you know that you have done enough learning?

What will the growth/success zone look like to you?

How will you know you have been successful?

What is the fear you harbour about changing this area of your life?

What fears might pop up in the learning and growth zones?

What might place you back into your original comfort zone and make you give up?

What could you do to overcome any setbacks?

On a scale of one to ten, ten being determined to achieve, and one being not bothered about this at all, how would you grade your determination to succeed at this goal?

Congratulations, another exercise completed. Don't worry if you didn't get as deep as you wanted with all your answers, you must do what suits, as long as it makes sense to you.

As I have mentioned previously, anything above a seven out of ten is a green light, so go for it. Anything below, suggests your heart isn't really in it, and perhaps the goal needs tweaking to make it more achievable. If at first you don't succeed, work out how to – use the TGROW model, look at your values, reward or bribe yourself, get a buddy or mentor to help you. Remember, if you give up, you are letting fear win and we can overcome fear. It's just a zone, a state of mind. Don't let it stop you from being the best version of you.

CHAPTER THIRTEEN

'The first and greatest victory is to conquer yourself; to be conquered by yourself is of all things most shameful and vile' – Plato

It's all very well ending up with an abundance of goals and intentions to better yourself, but if we don't check in with our life skills that will help us get there, then we are missing an opportunity to help the success along. I have my first 'proper' job at First Choice Holidays to thank for a lot of the skills I use to this day. Working as a holiday rep tends to spark the idea of sun-filled days on the beach, swanning around resorts and nights out on the lash living the high life. There are elements of truth there, but overall it's a very hard job that comes with long hours and as you are dealing with the general public, hundreds of them at a time, you are constantly being pulled from pillar to post in terms of looking after others. I can honestly say that my time overseas, and it was a five-year stint, did wonders for my life skills but naff all for my liver and self-care habits.

As a resort rep we were expected to: get to know the resort, the surrounding area, the accommodation (sometimes you had six or seven that you 'looked after'), local travel options, bus and train timetables, where the bus stops and train stations were, car hire prices, details of all the excursions, the best restaurants, takeaways, bars and supermarkets, the local market details, your hoteliers or apartment staff including cleaners (especially cleaners, if you have a room that needs getting ready in a flash, these guys and gals become the difference between a good relationship with your holidaymaker and a bad one). You needed to know the local customs, the shop times, where the post office was and its opening times, which banks had the best exchange rates and how to set up and prepare cabarets, create activities for bad weather, liaise with clinics, hospitals and doctors, know about sunburn treatment, where to avoid jellyfish, the best and worst beaches, the best bird-watching spots, enough about the archaeological ruins in the locality to get by, the best walks, the dangers of high tides.

Need I go on? It was immense. I was twenty-one years of age when I landed in Estartit on the Costa Brava for my first year and as I was in a resort with my manager an hour and a half away, I really was on my own.

That first year set me up for life. The transferable skills and experience were extensive. A rep's salary was shockingly low – in order to eat we lived on our commission, so we sold. Car hire, excursions and events around the resort that we set up ourselves: meals out, bowling nights and the aforementioned reps' cabaret. Actually, my first year didn't include that one, as I was on my own. But I did do a mean bar crawl whereby I had free drinks for me and a first free drink for each client, that needed negotiation, so my sales skills were essential in order to survive. Organisation was imperative – I couldn't visit all my accommodations, report problems and follow up relying on my memory alone – not with a hundred guests in resort.

Using a diary and a 'to do' list saved my sanity and kept the guests happy. We had to write weekly reports stating how things were going so that if guests complained when they got home there was a record. At that time (1989) there was no email, everything went onto paper and into a bag and onto a flight to Gatwick, our head office was near the airport. Calls overseas were very expensive, so paper it was, my spelling, grammar, ability to write professionally and succinctly was important.

With welcome meetings to hold, guest numbers to book in and rooms to check, the time just before the arrival of flights was very busy, then you had all the airport runs, some in the middle of the night. Managing your time so that you didn't burn out was imperative. I used to try and sleep a couple of hours each afternoon to catch up, as most nights I was out with guests. We had only one day off a week and the rest of the time you worked pretty much all day and all night. I can now see why this career suited the twenty-one-year-old brigade. You needed energy and stamina – that was another thing you learned to build up.

We had to declare all our sales, and so paperwork in the form of 'liquidation' was needed, if the money you had taken didn't add up, it could look as though you were stealing so you had to be methodical about traveller's cheques, cash in two currencies, (the country you worked in and sterling) and credit card payments which meant you must keep a record of each transaction. These were, of course, excellent money skills to have. Each week you would work out your commission, for most of us that was our motivation for doing the paperwork. At times I came across reps who struggled with figures and the mess they got into was awful. Always short on money, making up that shortfall out of their own pocket.

Then you had to keep an eye on the fact that your primary role was to look after the guests. This took some heavy-duty customer care skills, especially for those who were more challenging. Some would take delight in making your life as tricky as possible. A customer once told me that I had better do what was asked and pretty damn quick as he was 'paying my wages'. He had been hounding and baiting me from day one and he must have caught me on a rare off moment as my response was instant – he could have a refund of that salary he paid, I handed him the equivalent of about £1. He soon left me alone after that. So I guess you also learned when not to take any more rubbish.

Being assertive is the way to survive season after season with people who seem intent on trying your patience. In five years, he was the only guy I actually gave up trying to please. For everyone else, I went above and beyond the call of duty and it showed in the questionnaire results I got. I can now also see that this stint overseas may also have made me into a bit of a people pleaser.

Overall, my time looking after holidaymakers was one of the most amazing experiences of my life. It's hard to find a job that uses so many skills and demands so much of you as a person. I have missed my time often, but those attributes have been utilised again and again and set the tone for my future roles. So, over to you, what skills and experience can you identify from your earliest volunteer roles, jobs or even the position you are in amongst your family or friends? Take time to write them here, and consider the following questions which should help you.

> Think about as many previous or current roles as you can. Ask yourself which skills you acquired or what experience you gained. Write them out.

> What skills or experience do you think you need to help you achieve your goals/ways you wish to change/improve or develop yourself?

> Do you already possess them all? Some of them? Which ones, list them here.

> What can you do about the ones you might need?

In one of the last businesses I ran, I used to train other business owners in productivity skills. You probably have a whole range of these skills in your possession, so let's start with those you can identify, in other words what do you do and do well when it comes to organising yourself and getting stuff done? List them below.

Your productivity skills:

1.
2.
3.
4.
5.
6.
7.
8.
9.
10.

Now, what are the areas that you feel you could improve upon?

Why is this?

What would be the benefit of improving in these areas?

Looking at the above list, ask yourself if these areas are something you think you can do or do you need to get some help or support from elsewhere? Could you learn these skills from another person? A podcast, website or book?

Pop your ideas down here:

I shall share with you some of the ideas and tips that I used to go through in the productivity course that I ran – these are not in order of importance, just a range of suggestions, and you can select which work for you. Have a read through and think about what order you might use the ideas in, how might they help you to get your stuff done?

- **Identify what needs doing.** I tend to journal or scribble on paper first to empty my head of all the stuff rushing around inside. I love mind maps and if you have yet to use these check out the website for Tony Buzan, the creator of mind maps, there you can learn more and download free resources. If you put his name and 'mind maps' into YouTube, there are some five-minute videos there too. [14] The key is to start with *everything* you need, want or must get done. Word of warning however, if you include all you need to do (which you really should) this can look totally overwhelming. The good news is it's *out of your head* and that's liberating. As I have said to my students (and clients for that matter) how do you eat an elephant? Bit by bit. Get it all out of your head and into one place, then we can look at how to deal with it.

- **Eat the frog**. Mark Twain famously said that each morning you should eat a live frog, this was meant to be a productivity tip not a breakfast suggestion. If you get the worst task out of the way first thing, the rest of your day will surely be easier in comparison. Brian Tracey wrote an international bestseller called *Eat that Frog*, I have heard

[14] tonybuzan.com

great things about it. It makes sense to get the hardest, easiest to avoid task out of the way first thing, you will feel amazing for tackling it and the rest of the day's undertakings will appear less revolting in comparison.

- **Be clear on what's actually important and urgent.** I have a tendency to use amounts of time on tasks that I find less hard, enjoyable even, and, therefore, leave the important stuff. I procrastinate, basically. One way to be clear on what's urgent is to understand what you need to achieve. If you have your goal for the morning, day, week or your future in mind, write it on top of your list of things to do, then you can set the tasks that take you towards achieving that goal. If you ask yourself, 'is this action taking me towards or away from my goal?' you can quickly identify the important tasks. Then simply crack on.
- **'To do' lists**. I am a devil for having 'to do' lists all over the place. I scribble on pads, sticky notes, scraps of paper, magnetised lists on the fridge, plus notes and reminders in my phone – it could appear chaotic. But I am aware that in about twenty to thirty minutes I can sit and sift through the lot and create a 'to do' plan for the month, week, day, morning and hour. My brain likes the volume of information, but it also really loves one final list. I use the final list and I adapt it as priorities change. I also set an amount of time to work per day. If you are able to manage your time, remember to do things other than work. Exercise, cooking food from scratch, reading a few pages of a book, meditating, calling a friend, whatever you need to break up the day so you have a range of activities. If you are an employee you might have set breaks and a lunch hour, how can you make that free time as good as possible for you?

Write some ideas for some 'me time' during a busy work day down here:

- **The pomodoro technique** is one I use to this day, it's simple – you set a timer for twenty-five minutes, then work on one task until the timer goes off. Then you take a five- minute break. If you are stuck on a task, like writing for example, just getting twenty-five minutes of activity can kick start you and break the 'writers block'. Personally, I prefer fifty minutes on task, with a ten-minute break. You need to do what works for you. It is not productive to slave away on tasks for hours and hours without breaks, so please give yourself (and your brain) a rest regularly. If you work on a computer, your eyes will also thank you for regular time not staring at a screen.
- **Multitasking**. Oh, how I used to love this. I was constantly flitting from task to task, it seemed that my brain loved the variety and the feeling that I wasn't stuck on only one thing, I had another waiting. I used to spend all my time jumping around tasks. Then a friend came to help with a launch party I was running and he simply couldn't work with me. He is a professional person who I have the utmost respect for, so I listened when he started to question my thinking about multitasking. At this time, everyone was multitasking and I thought that he was crazy to not see the joy and wonder in bouncing around jobs. It turns out he was simply ahead of his time. Science supports his theory that it's ineffective, and staggeringly

there is proof that only 2.5 per cent of people do it well. I now focus on one thing at a time. If you like the variety of your workload, you could use the pomodoro technique and stay on a task for twenty-five minutes then switch, the evidence is out there to suggest we get more done with focus, and if you think about it, it does make sense. It's also quite tiring for the brain to chop and change so much.[15]

- One of the most dramatic improvement techniques I have ever heard about is the regularity of **checking email.** I have watched people in the workplace stop conversations when the alert pulls their attention to an email freshly landed in their inbox. The suggestion that you only check email three times a day can for some people be too uncomfortable to even consider. If you want to be productive and manage your time well, it's simply the way forward. If someone is so desperate to get hold of you, they will call. If you checked your email at the start of your working day, halfway through and then an hour or so before you finish up, based on a regular eight-hour work day, you will have been on your email every two to three hours.

  You can set up an automatic reply stating that you are checking email intermittently and if it's urgent to either contact a colleague or call you. Personally, I don't think it's unreasonable to let people wait for you to respond. You might be in a three-hour meeting, or travelling with no internet connection for that period of time. If you clear email three times a day, you will see what's a priority and fit it into your work schedule. You might need time to

---

[15] There's a good article about this here: forbes.com/sites/douglasmerrill/2012/08/17/why-multitasking-doesnt-work/#40d2c64d6ada Link to Brain Tracey, Eat That Frog https://amzn.to/2TUUtAT

contact someone with help or advice, then get back to the person. It's actually really empowering to not have emails distracting you every time they arrive. If you check and clear in one sitting, you are more likely to be in the zone, and not mid-task when they distract you. Try it, it saved me hours of time that I wasn't using productively as I was getting stuck in 'email busy' rather than 'what I needed to do' busy. I also file every single email after I read it, those that stay in my inbox rarely go above five in number, and they are there to remind me that they need action.

- **Understand when and where you work best.** If you are most productive first thing in the morning, then work then. If you need a few hours to get going, plan your trickier work for when you feel best able to tackle it. Save the lighter, less complex chores for times you know your energy levels and focus are lower. You might want to plan your day to allow time to exercise, you definitely need time to eat and switch off, I know people who eat at their desks whilst checking work. In some cultures this is considered the height of craziness. And speaking of desks, is that your best place to work? Or is it on the sofa? In bed? Outside? At a cafe? In a library? Consider your environment as that can really enhance how you feel about work. Need scented candles and flowers? Me too. I love a nice space to work in – it makes me feel happier. So work where you feel at your best.
- I tend to **split the day** into three sections when I am in control of my hours. Rise about 6 a.m., then start working about 6.30 a.m. with tea, laptop and still in my bed in my pjs and dressing gown. Stop after fifty minutes – see previous mention of the pomodoro technique. Grab some breakfast – away from my laptop. Start again for another fifty minutes. At some point, I'll take a longer break to shower and dress then return to my computer. At about 12 noon, I will have worked about four hours. The morning

> session always involves creative stuff – planning and writing. I take an hour or so for lunch, always something from scratch and as healthy as possible, then I get out of my home for a walk or a cycle ride. By the time the afternoon starts again around 2 p.m., I know I have another three hours and I choose tasks that are more research-based, gathering information, making calls, etc. This is also a good time for admin. If I need to, I'll work an eighth hour, but I tend to stick to seven hours working per day, which means I then have a lot of time to do things such as read, go to the gym and cook. You may have noticed that in the given example, I have chunked together similar tasks. This is less tiring for the brain. Massive switches from tasks can make your brain sluggish and you struggle. Not taking breaks can have that effect too. So, please do take breaks, you will be more productive, I promise you.

How about you? When you can manage your time and plan your activities, what do you think a typical day would look like? Plan it out now and add everything you have to do and that you want to do. Remember to be kind to yourself, burning out through overworking isn't fun, so best to avoid it by being kind to yourself now, get into good healthy work habits and you will increase your productivity. Try it and tweak your plans to fit you best. You might not get it right the first time, I didn't, not by a long shot. We are, after all, a work in progress.

Write your daily plan here:

As I get up at 6–7 a.m. and go to bed at 9–10 p.m., I know that I will be awake for fifteen hours. I work for seven hours, so I have eight hours a day for 'me time'. Personally, that is a good work–life balance, I have more time to myself every day than I give to my paid work. That feels right for me. In that 'me time' I might need or choose to do any of the following: write, research, shower, clean my home, travel, work out, eat, read, meet friends, meditate, watch television, cook. Knowing what I need or choose to do that day means I feel like all the projects I am working on are getting attention, I am looking after myself and I enjoy the feeling of moving towards completing my goals. You on the other hand, might prefer a more relaxed and less structured approach. You must do what works for you, as that's the only way you'll stick with it and feel good.

Knowing your time thieves is also very useful. If you have little people at home, it might be that your time gets taken up with the all-important role of childcare. I have a sister who gets up to exercise at 5.30 a.m., she loves that time of day when it's just her and her dog running miles in the early morning. This would feel like torture for me, but as we are all different, find what works for you. It might be that you can vanish into Facebook (other social media are available) for hours upon end. My biggest time thief is boxsets on Netflix and BBC iPlayer. If I get hooked, and let's face it, these programmes are designed and written to do exactly that, I will lose hours at a time. Therefore, I have a set screen time policy each night and I stick to it, otherwise nothing would ever get done.

Let's get you working on you again, here is another exercise to think about.

What are the things that steal your time?

And what could you do to avoid them?

If you can't avoid them, what could you do to work with them? Can you set time limits for example?

Well done on doing that, your answers can always be added to if you want to come back and review these exercises at any point.

CHAPTER FOURTEEN

'We are what we repeatedly do. Excellence, then, is not an act, but a habit' – Will Durant

I was reading about habits recently, in a library book (which I couldn't finish, sorry it was dragging its heels and not getting to the point in four chapters so I gave up) and went on good old Google.[16] Scientific evidence suggests that making something automatic is the best way to create a new habit. That makes sense, I think we all know that. What I didn't know was that new habits can take anywhere between eighteen and two hundred and fifty-four days to form. There is an oft quoted 'magic number' of twenty-one days needed to make a habit, but there is evidence to suggest that this is a misquote and I think the above parameter feels far more realistic. Afterall, we are all very different and how you form a habit compared to the way I do is likely to be poles apart. I think we also need to consider motivations when it comes to how long a habit takes to create. Let's take a look at the **good habits** you have made, can you list ten good habits that you know you have?

Some examples might be that you make your bed each day, get to work on time or that you keep your car clean.

1.
2.
3.
4.

---

[16] jamesclear.com is a useful source of information

5.
6.
7.
8.
9.
10.

Can you now list ten **bad habits** that you have?

1.
2.
3.
4.
5.
6.
7.
8.
9.
10.

Looking at the second bad habit list, do your current goals plan to deal with them? If it's going to take between eighteen and two hundred and fifty-four days to create ten new habits and overcome everything on your list, that might feel a touch overwhelming so you might want to take them one at a time.

What is the first goal that you are choosing to work on (that comes from your list of ten bad habits)?

My first goal is:

The reason I have chosen this one is:

Now use the TGROW model to clearly outline the work you plan to do to reach your goal.

Topic:

Goal (SMART):

Reality:

Opportunity:

Way forward:

Don't forget to grade your motivation to this goal out of ten, remember anything lower than a seven indicates a lack of intention to work on the goal!

You could keep a goal journal and write down how you find each day – are some days easier than others to work towards your goal? It might be of interest to see when the goal is reached and you have created a good habit from the old bad one. I asked a friend who was here fitting a radiator how long he felt his habits took to form, and he said it depended if it was a good or a bad one, but he felt six months was about right for him which is 182.5 days.

It's worth having a look at motivation when it comes to habits, clearly if your motivation is low, it's harder to start and maintain habit-forming behaviour. Recently, I downloaded *Not a Diet Book* by James Smith. It is a catchy title and I am aware that I have a little weight to lose. I think diets are evil and I have tried just one in my entire life. It was called the 'boiled egg and grapefruit diet' and I attempted it for three whole days when I was twenty-one years of age and knew no better. The fact I lasted just three days speaks volumes. I must have realised what a twit I was being and just stopped. The thing is, there are millions of diets out there and the weight loss industry is worth billions. It's a very confusing arena. Fortunately, James Smith has a brilliant down to earth approach to fitness and weight loss, so I have happily stuck with his book and just as I was writing this section on habits, I happened to read his thoughts on the subject. I recommend the book for a good educational read and a bit more clarity on food and exercise.

My personal motivation to lose a little weight is quite high because it's not very much, half a stone, so to me it feels very achievable as I have put on that amount before and lost it quite easily. On the other hand, I am not very motivated to exercise right now. I know that calories taken in need to be less than the calories I am burning off and for the past three months, that's not happened. My gym is closed due to Covid-19 restrictions and I dislike how busy the streets are when I try to go out for a walk or cycle. The city of Brighton and Hove is inundated with visitors, despite the pandemic, I think we have the beaches to thank for that. I have become quite the hermit and this lack of movement has caused the weight gain. I tried online yoga and pilates, zoom classes too, but I have failed to keep any kind of exercise routine going. It's unlike me to be so slovenly, and so I have resorted to bribery. It always works. But to reach this conclusion I took the following route, if you have a block about meeting a goal of yours, you might like to try it too.

First, I mind mapped why I am not exercising at the moment. What the blocks are. What my excuses are. Where my time is going instead, and how I feel about it.

I admitted to myself that I am being lazy, I am missing the gym, not really liking the YouTube videos I have found, my bike is broken and awful to ride, I prefer to read books, I love boxsets and I hate being outside where people aren't socially distancing and I dislike getting wound up at these people each time I go out. I would like to exercise as I miss it and I am disappointed that anything I do (like walks with friends) doesn't feel enough.

Secondly, I praised myself for all I have done that has been positive, where I should be kind to myself and congratulate myself. I looked at where I am using time well and what I am proud of. I came up with the fact that I am writing this book, that I have given up alcohol, I have become vegetarian, I have mediated daily for three months, I gave up dairy (on expert advice), I got my finances sorted out and saved up for the first time ever, I also did lots of research for this book, I started job hunting, looked at how to go about relocation and noted that I have in fact exercised, just not regularly and not enough.

The order of these two activities is important, I ended up feeling proud of myself rather than down on myself. From this positive mindset I was able to move to the third stage.

Stage three looked at the exercise methods I enjoy. These are: going to the gym, cycling, walking, pilates and yoga. The gym is closed, so I took my bike to be fixed. I was worried it would be expensive, the previous quote for a service was £130, and as the bike originally cost £170, I felt it wasn't worth it. However, I missed cycling so when a colleague mentioned a place in Brighton called Cranks which is a workshop that works on a donation basis, I made an appointment and had all the work done for far less than that quote. I was also supporting a not-for-profit community enterprise and being greener by getting on my bike and off buses. I love walking with friends – during the pandemic a socially-distanced walk with a friend has been a real treat. I want to keep doing these and have two or three people who love to walk for an hour plus with me. So far, so good – cycling and walking. Pilates is good for me as it helps my back and is fantastic for core strength, so I decided to follow a friend's YouTube recommendation for a twenty-five-minute class.

Having worked out what I could realistically do, I now needed to bribe myself to do it. It wasn't happening without a reward, so it had to be done. I knew I was going to be starting from doing pretty much no exercise so I needed to create a gentle first step. I set a goal of walking for an hour, plus a cycle of twenty minutes and one pilates class of twenty-five minutes for week one. It's a pretty low bar in terms of what I am capable of, but I am still giving myself £10 when I achieve it. After week one, I shall sit down and re-set the amount of exercise, I plan to increase both the cycling and pilates. Week three – well, I will create that when the time comes. It is easy, but as I do the exercise and feel good about having done it, it will increase my motivation to do more. I am deliberately setting myself up to succeed. That's how I create my good habits and break my old ones. I hope the ideas laid out are useful for you.

Do you know what motivates you? If we recall the principle of moving away from pain and towards pleasure, then the questions to answer might be some or all of the following:

> What causes you pleasure? Why is this? Write out your answer in as much detail as you can.
>
> Is it peer approval?
>
> Attainment of a qualification?
>
> Being able to see a physical result?
>
> Better health?

More money?

Proving to yourself you can overcome something?

Buying an item of importance to you?

More sleep?

Less stress?

Whatever your pleasure, make sure you know what you need to use to motivate you, and take little steps to start and maintain the work needed. You will get there if you continue to take steps, you will fail if you give up. It's as simple as that. And give yourself permission to take your time, habits are formed after up to two hundred and fifty-four days of effort, so off you go, enjoy the journey.

Book mentioned is by James Smith, *Not a Diet Book*
https://amzn.to/3z2y4Av

CHAPTER FIFTEEN

'What you think of yourself is much more important than what other people think of you' – Seneca

I don't recall the exact time in my life that I stopped trying to please others all the time and started focusing on pleasing myself, but it wasn't all that long ago. For so many years I was clearly putting what other people thought of me before what I thought of myself. When was that magic defining moment when I realised that this was pretty futile behaviour? I wonder what caused that revelation? Perhaps it was when I became more confident in my abilities and no longer sought approval? Could be. As soon as I became aware that I wasn't actually happy going along with whatever it was in order to please another, I stopped. I didn't feel a dramatic fall out, but over time, I simply didn't see certain people as much, because I knew there was now a disconnect where I would have opposing ideas and they, not me, found it hard for me to have a different opinion. I would continue to see them, just less often and when in their company, I would choose my words carefully to indicate that I wasn't going to simply fall in with their views.

Some useful statements I have used include:

- 'I can see your point' – short but sweet and can in no way be seen as argumentative.
- 'Well, we are all different, I guess others might not see it that way' – here you are not saying you disagree, this group of others might though.

- 'That's interesting, I haven't heard that point of view before' – a simple acknowledgment of their view, with absolutely no agreement.

Do you have people in your life that seem to want to monopolise and influence the conversation rather than allow lots of differing thoughts and views? Do you find yourself tired with this and wish it to stop? It's tricky if they are quite overpowering, but with some carefully chosen remarks, you can lessen the feeling that you have to agree with them. Being assertive does not mean that you are aggressive, you are sticking to your boundaries, however new they may be.

It's OK to care for others and be mindful of their voice and opinions, but not to the detriment of your own. It's all too easy to allow others who we respect and trust to influence us, but there has to come a point when we grow, that we realise we have our own voice to use and develop. I have some people in my life who, when I listen to and observe them, I can see that they go along with whoever or whatever is the most dominant voice and opinion in the room. These are very easy-going individuals who never ruffle feathers and play the peacekeeper role. They are diplomatic and tactful and I admire their ability to not say what's really on their mind. But remove them from that environment and it becomes clear that they do have strong opinions, but they 'don't want the hassle or argument' of voicing what they think.

I have devised the following set of questions to get the answers that I most certainly needed, and this process might help you too. If not required, feel free to jump to the next more relevant part of the book.

Why was I trying to please others?

In what way did I try to please others?

How did I stop doing what I wanted in order to please others?

What was the reward in doing this?

What was the cost to myself in terms of doing this?

What was my motivation for doing so?

Did I get a pay-off that made it worthwhile? If so, what?

At what point did I realise it wasn't worth it?

What prompted that?

How did I stop pleasing others?

What were the benefits to myself?

Were there any consequences for my change in behaviour?

Do I have any regrets?

If so, what might I do to work on those?

Well done for completing that, it's quite eye opening to look at this area. Awareness is the first step to dealing with things, in my opinion. I have to say that I am grateful for any difficult people who have appeared in my life over the years, they have shown me who I do not wish to be.

CHAPTER SIXTEEN

'The secret of change is to focus all of your energy, not on fighting the old, but on building the new' – Dan Millman

The dictionary says that change is 'to make or become different'. I define change as any external or internal thing that needs our attention and isn't what you are doing right now. Mine is a looser definition and intentionally so, I suggest that change happens minute by minute, hour by hour. So I wonder why it is that most of us seem resistant to change? That it feels scary and even stressful, overwhelming and causes a lot of us to simply stick our heads in the sand and ignore what needs doing. I have met many people who do everything in their power to avoid change, ignoring and hoping it'll go away and not need their attention. To the outsider they appear to be OK, but on closer examination, particularly when in a coaching session for example, how they feel about not making changes shows that they feel stuck, lacking, resistant and frightened. In some (OK, most) cases, instead of addressing this, the person simply stays in denial that change is what's needed and they continue to block out their feelings.

I recently read a blog that was shared on the Psychology Today website which offered some interesting insights.[17] Clearly, we resist change because of fear, it might be fear of failing at the thing we set out to do, it could be fear of being successful at it which might in turn bring a new set of problems. It could be that

[17] psychologytoday.com/gb/blog/the-adaptive-mind/201809/how-overcome-the-fear-change

we can't see the outcome of the change and, therefore, staying where we are feels safer. The brain is designed to keep us safe, so if you are resisting change, that's good news, your brain is working. So, if it's the brain's fault that we are staying in our comfortable place instead of branching out into a new unexplored territory, how do we get round that?

This book is all about ways to understand ourselves a bit more, to change, to be better, to grow and to develop, whether it's by teeny-tiny steps or by taking massive upheaval-style moves. We are all different, and we all want to move and grow at different paces. Working out what you want your story to be is a good way to allow the brain to follow the path of change. I like the book analogy – I studied literature for my degree and so had to read a different book each week, I love how authors tell stories and I particularly love how coaching clients tell their stories to me. In this exercise I want you to work out what your story has been so far, what it is now and what you want it to be in the future. I appreciate this sounds like a lot of hard work. That's not the intention. It should be fun, and if you think about it, quite easy. You have lived your life to this point, how would you summarise the plot of your story to now?

Write out your story so far, take your time, use a timeline if it helps, and by that I mean a line drawn from your date of birth to today's date, then simply mark off key events in your life along the line to trigger sections of the story. You might feel you don't need a timeline, perhaps a mind map would be useful? My tip here would be to just write and see what comes out – even if you only have ten or twenty minutes:

Great, well done for doing that, now you need to write down where you are today, what does this part of your story look like?

Finally, and hopefully, the easier part of the story to write (due to all the goal setting, TGROWing and other stuff you have covered thus far) is what you want your future story to look like. Be kind to yourself here, nothing you write here is 'set in stone', just outline your dreams, aspirations, hopes and goals, and think big, really try to go for it, allow that mind to get to grips with some high-aiming stuff that makes you feel excited and enthusiastic about your future:

Brilliant work, this is important stuff. The more you can narrate what you want the future to be, the more the brain can absorb, this is why visualisations are used so often in coaching and self-development. If you can create pictures and movies in your head that feel real and authentic, then you will start to feel like it's possible, a reality even.

Some things to remember about telling ourselves stories – they are private unless you want to share. They are chapters only, we can't continue a story until we turn the page, sometimes the changes we are wanting to make can be viewed as just a turn of the page. This can reduce them a little and perhaps make them less scary. Stories can change, how many times have you read a great book or watched a series or film and not seen a plot twist coming? If we view our lives in a story format, and it stands to reason that we are the author, then we are capable of 'writing' the story anyway we wish. If you haven't already done the exercises above, I would really recommend giving yourself time to do so. You deserve the kind of life that has been carefully thought out and crafted.

CHAPTER SEVENTEEN

'You can, you should and if you're brave enough to start, you will' – Stephen King

Are you a hoarder? I don't mean a hoarder that has 'so much stuff that you can only just open your front door and that you constantly risk landslides of possessions' type of hoarder, are you someone that holds onto stuff tightly and doesn't let go? It can be material, physical or it can be ethereal and non-tangible. I think we all are hoarders to a certain extent. I am currently listening to *The Art of Making Memories* and the author, Meik Wiking, goes into wonderful and fascinating research, facts and figures about nostalgia and recall of events, and it really got me thinking about the time last year that I got totally ruthless and threw away about eighty per cent of the contents of my loft.

Fast forward to this year and I cannot tell you how grateful I am that I did. I have had a dream about moving to either South East Asia or New Zealand, then Covid-19 happened and that put paid to that dream. I also had another reason not to fly out of the country. As I started this book I had a twenty-three-year-old cat. Billy was located via the wonders of the Co-op supermarket free notice board. I fancied a cat, the rescue home said I couldn't possibly have one of theirs as I was on the top floor of an old Regency building, and the cat would surely fall off the fire escape. Fast forward to 2020 and he hadn't fallen off anything for twenty-three years. I felt I should be his owner until he passed onto the big fire escape in the sky. This devotion has kept me in the UK, and quite right too. He was my cat and as he was old, a bit cranky and at times forgetting who was in charge (actually he has never known that) it was my duty to him to ensure I was by his side until the end and put up with his demands for food at 4 a.m. I wouldn't have wished that on anyone. Last year I thought as he was twenty-two, he might not be around too much longer, I might be able to take off for foreign shores and so I decluttered the loft.

I have Marie Kondo to thank for helping, she didn't actually pop round and get into the loft with me, but she did appear on Netflix and after watching two or three episodes of *Tidying up with Marie Kondo*, I was addicted to her philosophy. I then read her amazing book, *The Life-Changing Magic of Tidying up: The Japanese Art of Decluttering and Organising* and I began the declutter to end all declutters. If you have any old boxes, stacks of CDs, clothes, bags, shoes, etc. kicking about and you don't feel motivated to sort it out I highly recommend the Marie Kondo approach. It cleansed my belongings and my mind. As you let go of things, you actually feel a weight lifting. I opened a letter from the charity shop that received the stuff I cleared out, I had helped them raise hundreds of pounds, and that feels rather good too. The reason I mention Wiking's book is that nostalgia was the reason I had held onto all that stuff, Kondo was the reason I detached from everything that didn't give me any joy, and more importantly, was never going to be used or read again. I must have had half the Amazon rainforest up there in paper form – old letters, old journals and old books. I recycled the letters, I gave away the books and the journals stayed. I will read them in my old age and have a good old chuckle at the ridiculousness of my younger self.

Letting go of stuff actually led me to start thinking about what else to let go of, not immediately, just over the course of time. Add a clear mind (due to leaving alcohol alone) and a determination to make the most of the time I have in the UK, because I thought the way that cat is going, I might be here for some time. I have let go of a lot of personal stuff as well as material, so I want you to seriously consider these questions and answer as honestly as you can:

> Am I holding onto possessions that I have not looked at, worn or used in some time?
>
> If the answer is yes, list what these things are:
>
> Do I have clutter, either in view or out of sight that I am ignoring?
>
> If the answer is yes, list what these things are and where they are.
>
> Does my life feel cluttered in other ways?
>
> If the answer is yes, list where life feels cluttered.
>
> What would the benefits be, to let go of clutter either physical or non-tangible?
>
> Who can help me with this task?

Where can I go for support if I find this hard?

What will the reward be for doing so?

What do I want the outcome to look, sound or feel like?

How will I know I have achieved what I set out to do?

How shall I celebrate the work that needs to go into this?

What will I do with the money I make from selling this old stuff?

If you can get excited about the outcome, it tends to spur you on to make it happen. Letting go might start with the material and physical, but you start to realise that the action of letting go does help you mentally release too. Try it. As Marie Kondo advocates, you do not start with the emotional memory-laden stuff first. You start with the impersonal and work your way to the photograph albums and love letters. I would be doing her amazing work a disservice if I tried to share anymore, as I said she has a series on Netflix (if you don't fall in love with her I shall be amazed), books and a website.[18]

I want to end this book by focusing on what, to me, is the most important value I have: balance. When I sat in that doctors being

[18] Marie Kondo's official site is konmari.com and the book link is here: https://amzn.to/3xvW9zp

signed off work for three months, I was told I needed 'me time' and balance. But what does balance mean? I think it's a very subjective thing and we would all answer that question in a myriad of ways. I want to leave you the questions and exercise that I have identified as key to working on balance.

- Do you know where your time goes? If you answered yes, then that's great – where? Write out your daily plan from the minute you wake up – write it all down, think through your day and detail where your time goes. Eating, travelling, shopping, childcare, household chores, working, the gym, etc. (This might be easier to create on a laptop or PC so you can copy and paste, but as you know by now, I advocate the pen and paper approach as it aids the cognitive process.)
- Do this for as many days as you can – until you have built a realistic picture of where your time is going. Do a whole month if you need to. Looking at that daily plan over time can be eye opening. You might be happy with where your time is currently going, or horrified.
- If you are horrified, what do you need to change? Is there balance in your daily life? Are you getting time to do what you need to do? See friends? Exercise? Read? Go to that yoga class? Meet new people?
- Write down all that needs changing. Try to change just one thing at a time, if you take on too much, it might be overwhelming and you will give up so choose the pace you want to move at and do that.
- You could TGROW your new change, choose a reward and get support to make it happen.

As I am keen on saying to my students, we all have the same number of hours in the day. It's what you do with them that counts and makes all the difference. We know fifteen minutes of exercise, meditation or calling your mum is easy to fit in really, it's only fifteen minutes, but do we always do it? It's a choice we make at the time. If we are focusing on balance though, we might have it placed in a schedule, set a reminder on our phone or have it written on a sticky note.

As I mentioned before, I believe in carving up my day. I currently work part-time and set my own hours, I get up about 6 am, and I know I go to bed about 9.30–10 p.m. So I have about fifteen hours where I am awake. Each day. If I am on a 'non-working' day, I can choose to do absolutely nothing. And sometimes I do – I eat carrot cake, drink far too many oat milk lattes and read books all day long. Bliss. On the other hand, if I have a book to write, meditation to do, yoga to attend and an annoying 'to do' list, I carve up my day. I take twelve of the fifteen hours. Then I divide by four, are you with me so far? I end up with four chunks of three hours. I allocate half to the 'to do' list and half to me.

So today could look like this:

6 a.m. to 8 a.m. – wake up slowly, tea/breakfast in bed, catch up on social media/read
Chunk one: 8 a.m. to 11 a.m. – tackle the 'to do' list
Chunk two: 11 a.m. to 2 p.m. – 'me time' – read, write, eat, exercise, shower
Chunk three: 2 p.m. to 5 p.m. – go back to the 'to do' list
Chunk four: 5 p.m. to 8 p.m. – 'me time' – cook, call friends, meditate, work out, read, eat
8 p.m. to 9.30–10 p.m. – winding down with Netflix, iPlayer or a book and bath

If this style feels like something you might try, give it a go, or perhaps you need to tweak this model to give you more 'to do' time. Play around with it and see what suits you – there are lots of resources on the web to help plan time, please just remember, factor in some 'me time', get that balance, no one on their deathbed had regrets about not going to work more.

It's nearly time to say goodbye, as I think this book will give you enough to work on for now. I am planning to write more books, and I would love to have your company again. If you don't read much, I would encourage you to try as it can be escapism and we all need a bit of that now and again. The book I am still reading months later is *The Power of Now*, I am sorry, Mr Tolle, I know your book is a multi-million best-seller, loved by Oprah and many others, but wow, I have struggled, the complexity of the ideas just stops my brain in its tracks, I know I am resisting and for that reason, I know I need to read it. And I shall. The key message is that we only have now, and it's so true, I just find the other messages and explanations tricky but I shall get there and I highly recommend you try too. I know people who read it in one sitting, so please do not let me put you off.

I have Fearne Cotton's *Calm* on the go right now, her work is so accessible and I love the interviews she has on her 'Happy Place' podcast. I also have her journal of the same name. I write it up every day as you are supposed to and it is a little slice of 'me time' in the hustle and bustle of my life. I have three other books I am currently reading, but they are fiction, I think it's really important to have a balance of reading otherwise it might all feel like work, and we don't want that.

The things I have learned, the exercises I have used, the books, podcasts, websites and more are detailed throughout this book and I hope that you will go off and do your own searching around the subjects. I trust that this book helps, supports, inspires or nurtures the changes you need in your life in order to become the best version of you. Be patient and above all be kind to yourself, stay flexible, but focused, compromise when it's the best solution for you, be aware of those who are on side and those who might not be that healthy to have around as you change, celebrate the small and large steps, be kind to yourself (yes, I said that twice, for good reason) and take good care of your body. It's the only home you have when you think about it. Let your thoughts run wild, giggle at yourself, journal like crazy, come up with ideas, disregard any that feel wrong, trust yourself and above all get out of your own way. To conclude I wish to leave you a beautiful quote which is incorrectly most often attributed to part of Nelson Mandela's inaugural speech.

'Our deepest fear is not that we are weak. Our deepest fear is that we are powerful beyond measure. It is our light, not our darkness that most frightens us. We ask ourselves, who am I to be brilliant, gorgeous, talented, fabulous? Actually, who are you not to be?' This is taken from Marianne Williamson's 1989 best seller *A Return to Love*.

Finally, I will leave you with my deepest good wishes for your journey, and to thank you. For being brave enough to work on yourself. For that alone, you will always have my, and no doubt many others, respect. Jo – June 2021

P.S. Would you be kind enough to leave an honest review of the book where you bought it? As a new independent author, I am aware that this book will need other people like you to read it and appreciate it, so if you could share the word, others will get the opportunity to work on themselves too. Thank you very much.

P.P.S. Let's stay in touch! I am to be found on Facebook in my group We Are All a Work in Progress and at weareallaworkinprogress.co.uk – you are welcome to join my newsletter group which is a guaranteed short read, and a fabulous freebie awaits you for signing up.

Link to Fearne Cotton, Calm https://amzn.to/3ANI8yO

NOTES

Printed in Great Britain
by Amazon

71518536R00081